Andreas Herberg-Rothe (ed.)

Lessons from World War I for the Rise of Asia

**AN INTERDISCIPLINARY SERIES
OF THE CENTRE FOR INTERCULTURAL AND EUROPEAN STUDIES**

**INTERDISZIPLINÄRE SCHRIFTENREIHE
DES CENTRUMS FÜR INTERKULTURELLE UND EUROPÄISCHE STUDIEN**

CINTEUS · Fulda University of Applied Sciences · Hochschule Fulda

ISSN 1865-2255

10   *Volker Hinnenkamp / Hans-Wolfgang Platzer (Eds. / Hrsg.)*
     Interkulturalität und Europäische Integration
     ISBN 978-3-8382-0573-1

11   *Vera Axyonova*
     The European Union's Democratization Policy for Central Asia
     Failed in Success or Succeeded in Failure?
     ISBN 978-3-8382-0614-1

12   *Lisa Moessing*
     Lobbying Uncovered?
     Lobbying Registration in the European Union and the United States
     ISBN 978-3-8382-0616-5

13   *Andreas Herberg-Rothe (ed.)*
     Lessons from World War I for the Rise of Asia
     ISBN 978-3-8382-0791-9

14   *Agnieszka Satola*
     Migration und irreguläre Pflegearbeit in Deutschland
     Eine biographische Studie
     ISBN 978-3-8382-0692-9

Series Editors

Gudrun Hentges
Volker Hinnenkamp
Anne Honer †
Hans-Wolfgang Platzer

Fachbereich Sozial- und Kulturwissenschaften
Hochschule Fulda University of Applied Sciences
Marquardstraße 35
D-36039 Fulda
cinteus@sk.hs-fulda.de
www.cinteus.eu

Andreas Herberg-Rothe (ed.)

LESSONS FROM WORLD WAR I FOR THE RISE OF ASIA

ibidem-Verlag
Stuttgart

Bibliografische Information der Deutschen Nationalbibliothek
Die Deutsche Nationalbibliothek verzeichnet diese Publikation in der
Deutschen Nationalbibliografie; detaillierte bibliografische Daten sind im
Internet über http://dnb.d-nb.de abrufbar.

Bibliographic information published by the Deutsche Nationalbibliothek
Die Deutsche Nationalbibliothek lists this publication in the Deutsche Nationalbibliografie;
detailed bibliographic data are available in the Internet at http://dnb.d-nb.de.

Cover picture: Ernst Barlach, Der Fries der Lauschenden - Die Tänzerin, 1931, Eichenholz, Ernst Barlach
Haus, Hamburg. Photo: Rufus46. Source: Wikimedia Commons. Licensed under CC-BY-SA
3.0 (s. http://creativecommons.org/licenses/by-sa/3.0/deed.en).

∞

Gedruckt auf alterungsbeständigem, säurefreien Papier
Printed on acid-free paper

ISSN: 1865-2255

ISBN-13: 978-3-8382-0791-9

© *ibidem*-Verlag
Stuttgart 2015

Alle Rechte vorbehalten

Das Werk einschließlich aller seiner Teile ist urheberrechtlich geschützt. Jede Verwertung
außerhalb der engen Grenzen des Urheberrechtsgesetzes ist ohne Zustimmung des Verlages
unzulässig und strafbar. Dies gilt insbesondere für Vervielfältigungen,
Übersetzungen, Mikroverfilmungen und elektronische Speicherformen sowie die
Einspeicherung und Verarbeitung in elektronischen Systemen.

All rights reserved. No part of this publication may be reproduced, stored in or introduced into a retrieval
system, or transmitted, in any form, or by any means (electronical, mechanical, photocopying, recording or
otherwise) without the prior written permission of the publisher. Any person who does any unauthorized act
in relation to this publication may be liable to criminal prosecution and civil claims for damages.

Printed in Germany

Editorial

This series is intended as a publication panel of the Centre of Intercultural and European Studies (CINTEUS) at Fulda University of Applied Sciences. The series aims at making research results, anthologies, conference readers, study books and selected qualification theses accessible to the general public. It comprises of scientific and interdisciplinary works on inter- and transculturality; the European Union from an interior and a global perspective; and problems of social welfare and social law in Europe. Each of these are fields of research and teaching in the Social- and Cultural Studies Faculty at Fulda University of Applied Sciences and its Centre for Intercultural and European Studies. We also invite contributions from outside the faculty that share and enrich our research.

Gudrun Hentges, Volker Hinnenkamp, Anne Honer & Hans-Wolfgang Platzer

Editorial

Die Buchreihe versteht sich als Publikationsforum des Centrums für interkulturelle und europäische Studien (CINTEUS) der Hochschule Fulda. Ziel der CINTEUS-Reihe ist es, Forschungsergebnisse, Anthologien, Kongressreader, Studienbücher und ausgewählte Qualifikationsarbeiten einer interessierten Öffentlichkeit zugänglich zu machen. Die Reihe umfasst fachwissenschaftliche und interdisziplinäre Arbeiten aus den Bereichen Inter- und Transkulturalität, Europäische Union aus Binnen- und globaler Perspektive sowie wohlfahrtsstaatliche und sozialrechtliche Probleme Europas. All dies sind Fachgebiete, die im Fachbereich Sozial- und Kulturwissenschaften der Hochschule Fulda University of Applied Sciences und dem angegliederten Centrum für interkulturelle und Europastudien gelehrt und erforscht werden. Ausdrücklich eingeladen an der Publikationsreihe mitzuwirken sind auch solche Studien, die nicht 'im Hause' entstanden sind, aber CINTEUS-Schwerpunkte berühren und bereichern.

Gudrun Hentges, Volker Hinnenkamp, Anne Honer & Hans-Wolfgang Platzer

Table of Contents

ANDREAS HERBERG-ROTHE
World War I and the Current Conflicts in the World: An Introductory Essay 7

CHRISTOPHER COKER
(Ir)rational Actors: Why Great Powers Can Still Go to War 19

HARALD MÜLLER & CARSTEN RAUCH
Make Concert, Not War: Power Change, Conflict Constellations,
and the Chance to Avoid Another 1914 39

NAMRATA GOSWAMI
The New Major Powers of Asia: Will Their Strategic Choices and Preferences
Overshadow the West? Drawing Lessons from 1914 71

PANG ZHONGYING
China's Choice: Contributing to the Emergence of a Concert of Powers
in the Asia-Pacific 99

ANTULIO J. ECHEVARRIA II
Revisiting the First Modern Arms Race Leading to World War I:
Implications for the Asian Rebalance 119

ARTYOM LUKIN & ANDREY GUBIN
Eurasia's Emerging Geopolitics: Back to 1914? 135

About the Authors 161

References 165

Index 171

World War I and the Current Conflicts in the World – An Introductory Essay

Andreas Herberg-Rothe

All countries in the non-Western world have only one aim – to be recognized again as equal by the leading Western powers in order to regain their former status as world powers and civilizations, which was lost in the process of European colonization and subsequent American hegemony. The desire for recognition is the driving force behind the economic and political rise of Asia. The same was true with respect to the conflict between established, rising, and declining powers before World War I. Are there lessons to be learned for our times from the devastating conduct and outcome of World War I? Is there only one lesson to be learned – that you can learn nothing from history? Or are we doomed to repeat history if we learn nothing from it? History will not repeat itself precisely, but wars repeatedly occur throughout history, even great wars. We are living in an age in which a war between the great powers is viewed as unlikely because it seems to be in no one's interest, since the outcome of such a war would be so devastating that each party would do its utmost to avoid it. Rationality seems to dominate the assumptions and way of thinking in our times. But no war would have been waged if the losing side, or even both sides, had known the outcome in advance.

Historical analogies are not just a subject for historians or mere abstract – they form our way of thinking about how to deal with today's conflicts. The most important problem for the political discourse of our times is whether an analogy to the pre-World War I era or that of the pre-World War II era is appropriate for dealing with the current conflicts in the world. If we use concepts and strategies with the main aim of avoiding a repetition of totalitarian or imperialist movements and states, which led to developments similar to those resulting in World War II, a realist approach might be reasonable. This would mean rearmament, an arms race, deterrence, regime change, and even war to avoid a new world war. Writing this political discourse, John Bolton, former US Ambassador to the UN, emphasized: To stop Iran's bomb, bomb Iran (New York Times, March 26, 2015). But if the current situation more closely resembles the pre-World War I era, these strategies and policies to avoid a similar development leading to World War II would eventually lead to a repetition of World War I.

1914, the beginning of the First World War, has not repeated itself as the start of the First World War in Asia in 2014. But there are striking similarities between the pre-World War I era and the current developments in Asia: the one-hundredth anniversary of World War I signifies the danger, not the inevitability, of a new world war in the decades to come. World War I is a symbolic representation of the risk that a war amongst the great powers could erupt even though nobody would benefit from it. It is the writing on the wall that rationality does not guarantee avoidance of self-destruction. Although the 1914-2014 analogy has already passed, the more disturbing problem is marked by 1915 – the year in which a still-limited European war escalated into a world war.

All predictions regarding a repetition of World War I in Asia are based on the assumption that it would be in no one's interest to fight a large-scale war that could lead to the destruction of great parts of Asia, Europe, and North America (the presence of weapons of mass destruction also worsens the prospects). But what if conflicts in Asia would not be fought to pursue national interests so much as recognition? That is, to be accepted as equal again after the humiliation over the course of European colonization and subsequent American hegemony? Indeed, acknowledgment of past suffering seems to be a trauma on the conscience of many Asian nations. Are those desires irrational or simply a different kind of rationality that we have to take into account?

During her last visit to Beijing in September 2012, then-US Secretary of State Hillary Clinton held a press conference in which she stated that the world would soon see, for the first time in history, that a rising power and an established power would not engage in a war. Of course, her statement was related to China and the US. Additionally, she compared the competition between China and the US with that of the Peloponnesian War between Sparta and Athens – authoritarian Sparta against democratic Athens. Athens, the strongest city-state in Greece before the war, was reduced to a state of near-complete subjugation, while Sparta established itself as the leading power. Thucydides, the chronicler of the Peloponnesian War and one of the ancient world's most important historians, saw the initial cause of this war in the growth of Athenian power: "What made war inevitable was the growth of Athenian power and the fear which this caused in Sparta." Unlike Plato, though, Thucydides argues that it was not the striving for power in itself, but rather fear of losing power and, in the long term, fear of being oppressed, robbed of one's freedom, and enslaved that caused the escalation leading to war. In Thucydides's account, fear was the cause of war on both sides. Sparta was afraid of the growth of Athenian power and Athens was afraid of what might happen if it gave in to an escalating series of demands and threats without a foreseeable end.

No one wanted World War I to happen. Or, at least, no one wanted the kind of war that actually took place. The general assumption was that the conflict would be very limited. The Europeans who went to war assumed they would be home by Christmas 1914. We know now, of course, that World War I not only happened but that it also resulted in the self-destruction of the European powers in two world wars. World War I teaches the lesson that a limited conflict can escalate into a nightmare of millions of deaths and unspeakable suffering for which no rational explanation could be found. Military aims and strategies gained priority over meaningful political goals. Although the generals of the German Empire believed that they were relying on Clausewitz's theory, they actually perverted it. Tactics replaced strategy, strategy replaced politics, politics replaced policy, and policy was militarized. It was as if everybody was saying that being at war means we stop thinking.

Perhaps the deepest hidden reason for this escalation was that each war party could admit neither defeat nor failure. A striking piece of evidence for this assumption is that the proclaimed war aims of the German Empire gained momentum the more unrealistic and irrational they became. The pride, honor, and identity of the German Empire prohibited the acknowledgment of defeat and failure. The same was true for Russia, France, England, the Habsburg Empire, and the Turkish Empire. Perhaps these Empires especially knew that their rule wouldn't survive if they had to acknowledge military defeat or failure, as either would have ruined their identity and they would have lost "face" (social recognition within their society and community). A military defeat would signal their "symbolic death" – and so, the empires fought a war for life and death. This does not mean a simple equation of rising China with the then-rising German Empire. Although the actors then and today seem quite different, the dynamics generated by the conflict between emerging, rising, and declining powers are strikingly comparable.

Robert MacNamara, the US Secretary of State during the Cuban Missile Crisis, famously noted that it was sheer luck, not rationality, that prevented the escalation of that crisis into a world war. In 1983, the world needed more than good luck to avoid nuclear disaster. In the present day, all great powers are using military means to pursue their political and economic interests. But we simply should not allow ourselves to bet that military conflicts and strategies will not lead to the escalation of limited conflicts into great power wars.

The re-politicization of war and globalization

Since the end of the East-West conflict, terms like risk society, reflexive modernization, and globalization have been used in both academic and public debates as part of an intensifying discourse about how the accelerating transformation of social and national identities is affecting societies. Social, political, and economic developments devalue knowledge that has been handed down and traditional models of interpretation and give rise to a need for new perspectives.

Cultural and religious conceptions of order, in their special historical and contemporary contexts, were re-actualized for providing orientation to people in a quite dramatically changing world. As processes of change and transformations of their life-worlds affect people, they reconstruct and reorganize these conceptions of order so that they can comprehend and explain their changing world. In the way people build communities in order to defend and promote these different kinds of order, these aspirations become automatically political in essence. In a globalized world, these communities are becoming increasingly political, regardless of whether they exist for a long or short time or whether they seem to be determined by religion, culture, national aspirations, or a tribal background. The sole aspect of importance is that they are defending their identity and spreading their order and values as a community against or with others.

With these proposals, I do not want to draw into doubt some tendencies towards a privatization of war and violence in general (because they are appropriate for particular cases), but that current developments in the strategic environment display fundamentally conflicting tendencies: between globalization and struggles over identities, locational advantages, and interests; between high-tech wars and combat with "knives and machetes" or suicide bombers; between symmetrical and asymmetrical warfare. The conflict is also between the privatization of war and violence and their re-politicization and re-ideologization—conflicts over "world order"; between the formation of new regional power centers and the hegemonic dominance of the only superpower; between international organized crime and the institutionalization of regional and global institutions and communities; and between increasing violations of international law and human rights on one side and the expansion of international law and human rights on the other.

Liberal progress produces illiberal counter-reactions, and some political forces are pursuing a liberal order with elements that could be regarded as essentially illiberal. But the main distinction is whether we fight disorder and privatized violence or whether different kinds of order are in a conflicting competition.

This conflict becomes most apparent not only in the way in which we ourselves conceive the concept of victory, but even more importantly in which ways, for example, low-tech adversaries define victory and defeat. This is an exercise that requires cultural and historical knowledge about their political order much more than it does gee-whiz technology.

Robert Kaplan argued that the rules of war could only be applied against enemies with which we share a similar cultural background or at least a similar concept of rationality, but that the rules of the jungle must be applied to survive "new wars." This is fundamentally wrong because outside the "developed world," there is not one single jungle in which the Hobbesian war of all against all is the predominant kind of conflict. However, there are also extensive areas of the world in which violent conflicts about political, cultural, social, and even religious order are emerging. In the long run, these kinds of conflict will be prevalent. Robert Kagan argued that Europeans are from Venus, enjoying peace, whereas the US-Americans are from Mars and have to secure this peace by power-politics and even by force. But he admitted that this was not always the case and argued that until the beginning of World War I and Woodrow Wilson's presidency, these roles were reversed. But if this was the case, the paramount question remains: to which results for the European powers did their pure power politics before World War I lead? Nothing other than the self-destruction of Europe in World War I.

Conflicts about different kinds of order

After the collapse of the global system of order in the Cold War, most conflicts initially revolved around the contrast between order and disorder (as symbolized by concepts such as privatized violence, low-intensity conflict, and failed states). Since 1996, when the Taliban seized power in Afghanistan, different conceptions of order were at stake.

The German sociologist Max Weber emphasized that an order maintained for goal-oriented interests is much less stable than one that is respected "as a matter of custom arising from a settled behavioral orientation." This kind of order, however, is much less stable than "one which enjoys the prestige that follows from being seen as exemplary or binding; let us call this 'legitimacy.'" It is very nearly possible to synchronize Max Weber's classification of the different levels of stability of different orders, resting on interests, custom, or legitimacy, with the previous developments in warfare starting with the collapse of the Soviet Union. Immediately after the disintegration of the Soviet Union, wars related to private enrichment and the pursuit of interests were most visible. These were then gradually replaced by conflicts involving ethnic groups, the formation of small states, and national minorities. Finally, they were replaced by concepts of "world order" such as Islamism, which doesn't contribute to individual interests or ethnic rivalries.

Huntington's emphasis on cultural and civilizational conflicts between different conceptions of order captured one important aspect of ongoing developments, but he too mechanically treated these conflicts as taking place between civilizations, when in fact they are just as prevalent within civilizations, if not more so. But he was right in assuming that future conflicts are shaped by those conflicts concerning local, regional, or even world order, regardless of whether this particular kind of order is more related to culture or religion or "civilization."

These simultaneous processes of disintegration and reconstruction of order within communities are in (often violent) conflict with those between many communities, as well as with the overall tendencies grounded in geopolitics and globalization. The key problem here is not the value we attach to our own conception of order, but the fact that the conflict dynamic obeys rules that differ from those operating in a paradigm where conceptions of order and anarchy confront each other directly.

Globalization

It is obvious in my view that globalization is intensifying conflicts over world order, which leads to the return of geopolitics of different great and even global powers. The main task, therefore, is to avoid the escalation of conflicts between old and new global powers (most of the latter are old empires, striving for their renewed recognition as world powers, which they have lost in the process of colonization) and to avoid an arms race that could eventually lead to new traditional wars, considering the unstable situation most noticeable in states like Pakistan and Ukraine, but possibly also in former empires such as India, China, and Russia.

Politics must not be reduced to power politics within or between states. The negative effect of one-sided power politics could be observed in the developments that led to World War I and in our times can be observed in the Israel-Palestinian conflict as well as in conflicts in failed states like Syria, Ukraine, Libya, and Egypt. Although the relation of policy and war as Clausewitz describes it did not change substantially, a globalized world does need a concept of policy and politics that fits the ongoing process of globalization. Clausewitz wrote: "It can be taken as agreed that the aim of policy is to unify and reconcile all aspects of internal administration as well as of spiritual values, and whatever else the moral philosopher may care to add. Policy, of course, is nothing in itself; it is simply the trustee for all these interests" – not against other states, as Clausewitz wrote in his time, but against the worldwide expansion of war and violent action within and between states.

In the past 20 years, we have witnessed expectations of revolution in military affairs (RMA) and the appearance of seemingly new kinds of warfare, the so-called "new wars." The RMA promised to present, to a serious extent, technological solutions for political conflicts. Warfare and "military operations other than war" seemed to be legitimate if they were easily won. The costs would remain limited and the adversary could be presented as an outlaw of the international community, in a classical view, as a dictator or warlord who would have no support from the majority of the populace. All three propositions proved fatally wrong in Afghanistan and Iraq. For a short period, this understanding of the current battle space was revived in the campaign against Libya and the interpretation of the Arab Spring through Western eyes, which are used to view communities as being composed of individuals whereas in most parts of the world society is composed as a "community of communities." This is more important as more technical opportunities are expected in 21st century warfare. To put it bluntly: the evolving battle space of the 21st century is about ethics and the morality of using force—its legitimacy. The more technical opportunities in warfare we develop, the more the morality of its use comes to the fore.

There are many structural similarities between the pre-1914 period in Europe and the current conflicts in Asia. History will not repeat itself exactly, but the resemblance is striking. There are good precautionary warnings from the comparison. Nevertheless, the task is no longer to discuss whether similarities or differences count for more. The real task is already to take precautionary steps now in order to ensure that no new world war will start in Asia. Here, Cold War efforts to avoid military conflict between the superpowers (such as the "hotlines" between Washington and Moscow) could be meaningfully applied to the current conflicts in Asia. As it stands, the lack of multilateral institutions – like those created in Europe after 1945 – to settle the disputes in Asia is in itself dangerous.

Hegel's notion about the importance of the struggle for recognition leads to the conclusion that intercultural communication is not only necessary with respect to relations between Europe and Asia, but perhaps even more important within Asia. A world war starting in Asia would not be about interests, but rather would be a cultural war for mutual recognition. Only intercultural communication and strong multilateral institutions are capable of avoiding the nightmare of a great power war in Asia, which would lead to a repetition of 1914. Globalization poses the same problem for modern warfare as the French Revolution and Napoleonic warfare did for the theory of war in their times. The eminent Chinese scholar Zhang Wei Wei has argued that the world is at a watershed for the transformation of a hierarchically structured international system to a more symmetrical one. Nevertheless, this proposition does not only have serious implications for the US, but also for China, India, and Russia. Based on Hegel's proposition of the "progress in the consciousness of freedom" and Zhang Wei Wei's observation, it could be said that we are at a watershed in world history: the transformation of merely hierarchical societal relations into more symmetrical ones between and within societies by ensuring the progress of freedom as well as the human right of equality.

The contributions collected in this volume attempt to identify the forces that could lead to a repetition of history and to outline measures and mechanisms that could contribute to the avoidance of such a nightmare. All the authors have different backgrounds; as tensions are mounting between their respective nations, they might well be viewed as representatives of those nations. But this would not do justice to their intellectual effort and the fact that despite their differences, they all share the desire to contribute to a development in which political and military conflicts don't escalate into a new world war. The aim of this anthology, therefore, is to initiate a discourse for the decades to come, in which despite our conflicting or competing interests, identities, and self-understandings, the obligation to develop policies and strategies in order to avoid the escalation of conflicts and competition in Asia into a new world war gains momentum.

Thomas Hobbes once famously noted that the natural state of mankind is not peace, but the war of all against all. We should not delude ourselves with the assumption that peace is the natural state of mankind in our age. The late Yitzhak Rabin made the proposition: you don't need to make peace with your friends, you need to make peace with your foes. Carl Schmitt believed that the essence of politics is the differentiation of friends and foes. In my interpretation of Hannah Arendt and Carl Schmitt, the differentiation of friends and foes is the initial proposition of politics, but its final aim is the mediation of friends and foes, to find a common ground *between* these antagonistic contrasts without eliminating the competition (this concept stems from Plato, Eric Voegelin and Hannah Arendt). This might be the most important lesson we should learn from history.

Acknowledgments

I'm more than grateful to the scholars from various countries who contributed to this volume by relying on my trustworthiness. This volume took shape in a process to which the following scholars additionally contributed, either by critique, recommendations, encouragement, or even by extensively editing English: Robert Dujarric, Rana Mitter, Joseph S. Nye, Emile Simpson, and Hugh White were of enormous help in different ways. Gaelen Strnat was essential concerning English editing. Nevertheless, all remaining faults remain my own as the editor of this volume.

This anthology contains in most part the proceedings of the symposium "Lessons of 1914 for the future of Asia" in Tokyo from July 14-15, 2014. I'm very grateful for the generous support and funding of this symposium by the German Embassy in Tokyo, the Institute of Contemporary Asian Studies, Temple University Tokyo, and the faculty of social and cultural studies, University of Applied Sciences, Fulda, and in particular for the support of our Dean, Prof. Heinrich Bollinger.

Ernst Barlach, "Das Wiedersehen" ("The Reunion")

Soldier releasing messenger pigeon from tank, World War I

(Ir)rational Actors: Why Great Powers Can Still Go to War

Christopher Coker

Abstract:

When discussing the prospects of Great Power war we only have one real analogy: World War One. The world stumbled into war in 1914 because the Great Powers thought it so improbable. The US and China are in danger of doing the same. The main lesson to be learned from the First World War is that the rational actor model is seductive, but misleading. War is not necessarily irrational, even if it may be unreasonable to think there will be a victor. We are not as rational as we think. We are moved by passions and sentiments. We are intensely ideational. Different societies have different worldviews as well as different rationalities, which often encourage different ways of thinking about war and peace. If we are to preach the virtues of peace we must also comprehend the attractions of war.

Keywords: First World War, Norman Angell, William James, Rational Actor, The Cool War

Inevitably, the analogy that everyone tends to draw upon when contemplating the improbable – a conflict between the US and China – is the outbreak of war in 1914. In many respects, the world on the eve of the Great War seems not so much the world of a century ago, as the world of today, curiously refracted through time. We are rightly fascinated by the many ways in which the world on the eve of the First World War, apparently so far distant in time, is paralleled in our own. And one of the reasons why historians are fascinated by the war is that so many leading thinkers felt another Great Power conflict to be as improbable as most commentators do today.

One of the leading figures in the "new school" of historians distinguishes three stances of the war's origins: inevitable, avoidable, and improbable. And she identifies the weakness of the last two. War would only have been "avoidable" if the political leaders had set out to do everything in their power to avoid it; they didn't, in part because they thought it so unlikely. And war would only have been "improbable" if they realized how, given the tinderbox of European politics, only remarkable crisis management skills could have kept the continent at peace. We must conclude that war was largely "inevitable" because the politicians didn't take its prospect seriously enough.[1]

These days, historians are reluctant to blame Germany exclusively for the war. They prefer to emphasize the long-term dynamics that set the stage for 1914, including intensifying economic and imperial competition; rampant nationalism in all countries, even liberal ones; Social Darwinist beliefs then strongly embedded even in popular culture; and an entangling system of alliances and first-strike strategies that made most of the Great Powers as much victims as aggressors. But one inescapable fact remains; in the last stages of the July crisis two countries decided on war as a solution to their systemic problems: Austria and Germany. There is no reason to think that the Germans were gunning for war when they gave Austria a blank check, but they were certainly prepared to live with the consequences in the firm belief that they were in a stronger position to win a war against Russia and France in 1914 than they would be in the years to come.

For a western writer, what is fascinating about the 1914 analogy is that the outbreak of war exploded one widely held proposition: that at least in the case of inter-state conflict, violent competition, to quote the father of Social Darwinism, Herbert Spencer, had "given all it had to give"; it no longer paid dividends on belief.

The Great Illusion

Perhaps the most famous writer to adopt this line was Norman Angell. Speaking to the Institute of Bankers in London in January 1912, Angell contended that:

> Commercial interdependence, which is the special mark of banking as it is of no other profession or trade in quite the same degree – the fact that the interest and solvency of one is bound up with the interest and solvency of many; that there must be confidence in the due fulfilment of mutual obligation or whole sections of the edifice crumble – is surely doing a great deal to demonstrate that morality after all is not founded upon self-sacrifice, but upon enlightened self-interest, a clearer and more complete understanding of all the ties that bind us the one to the other.

---

[1] Jack Beatty, *The Lost History of 1914* (London: Bloomsbury 2012), 4

A former editor of the *Financial Times* who was present at the meeting later reported that Angell had carried the audience almost to a man.[2]

Today we also live with the thought that the world is becoming ever more complex and war even less decisive as a result. We are not the first to discover complexity, although we always think of ourselves as being in the forefront of every major intellectual trend. Complexity, wrote Angell, defied the previous ordering power of war. He hammered home the point in a book called *Europe's Optical Illusion* (1909), though all subsequent editions were titled *The Great Illusion,* by which it is now widely known. One of his forecasts was that war would disrupt the flow of international credit. Merely the knowledge of this should be sufficient to deter it from being fought; even if war did break out, a credit crisis would soon bring it to an end. Angell insisted that international finance was so complex and the world so interdependent that "robbery" had become unprofitable and diplomatic "dishonesty" profitless.

To be fair, Angell had good reason to arrive at this comforting conclusion. By 1914, the advanced European economies had become part of a continent-wide business cycle which extended across the Atlantic, though the immediate impact was actually more limited than either he or his contemporaries recognized at the time. Governments might sign international postal, telegraphic, and wireless conventions and harmonize railway timetables, but they continued to preach protectionism and to engage in economic nationalism. And financial interdependence, contrary to what Angell claimed, did not make hostilities unthinkable. Ironically, the international bond market actually facilitated war finance when the conflict finally came.[3]

Angell was listened to, nevertheless, because he was tapping into a whole system of thought. This was the first time that people began talking about global networking, although they did not yet use the term. By 1900, the world had gone global. The 100 million Europeans who had emigrated from Europe to North America in the course of the nineteenth century were part of an Atlantic system. The massive movement of money across the Atlantic also produced a one-world economy. Prices for the first time converged across markets; interest rates converged as well. And for the first time, economic

---

[2] John Keegan, *The First World War* (London: Hutchinson 1998), 11-12
[3] David Stevenson,*1914-18: The History of the First World War* (London: Penguin 2004), 6

slumps quickly became worldwide as the world financial system came into being, one of the structures, as we have seen, on which Angell pinned his hopes for world peace.

But if Angell was at one with the received opinions of the time, he labored under several illusions of his own making, and we tend to forget what he was actually saying because few of the writers who still quote him have bothered to read his book. To begin with, it was not quite the peace tract that we tend to think. Angell took ideas seriously and that, in part, was the problem. They were *his* ideas (or rather the commonplace thoughts of his countrymen), and he chose to edit out everything that was not relevant to his own worldview. All he noticed were the risks, not the *opportunities,* of going to war.

He was also remarkably deaf to the case for war put by those who were critical of liberalism, especially in Imperial Germany. A particularly striking example is the famous address that Max Weber gave in 1895 on the occasion of his appointment to the Chair in Political Economy at the University of Freiburg. The science of political economy (a largely British invention), he told his audience, was a *political* science, and its only purpose was to extend the *national* economy of states. None of this was especially new; what was new was the aggressive language in which he couched his argument. His address was peppered with words such as "survival" and "selection" and expressions such as "historical" laws and the "struggle of nations," all taken directly from the vernacular of Social Darwinism. Similar thoughts can be found in the writing of Weber's contemporaries such as Werner Sombat, who took issue especially with Spencer's belief that war had "given all it had to." It was, he considered, typical of the "self-satisfied" spirit of a country that had achieved industrial pre-eminence first. When war with Britain eventually broke out, Sombat complained that "often we can't help but feel we are fighting not a country, but a department store." [4]

Perhaps it is a little unfair to suggest that the belief in liberalism and progress was not only a casualty of war; it was also one of the war's causes. But the liberals can certainly be accused of a heavy dose of wishful thinking. In the end, anyway, Germany chose the path of war. Historians still ask why – the struggle for markets, nationalist sentiment, or domestic political pressures? All these played a part, to be sure, but none of these material factors usually "cause" war. They simply set the frame of reference in which the struggle will

---

[4] Hans Joas and Wolfgang Knöbl, *War in Social Thought* (Princeton NJ: Princeton UP 2013), 4

be fought. What really produces conflict is a society's emotional response to violence and what it expects to gain from going to war, hence the importance of Social Darwinism. If enough people tell themselves that war is a necessary part of the struggle for existence, a biological necessity of the first importance (that "to supplant or be supplanted is the essence of life";[5] if war is accepted as the stage or staging ground on which a nation can fulfil its "historical purpose"), then material explanations become rather superfluous.

The same, I would hazard, is true for societies that conclude that everything is to be gained from peace and nothing from war. Angell's ideas were all the more influential for being grounded in a system of thought that was largely unacknowledged. He firmly believed, for example, that the British Empire offered the ultimate behavioral model for humanity.

> It is to English practice ... and experience that the world will look as a guide in this matter ... The extension of the dominating principle of the British Empire to European society as a whole is the solution of the international problem which this book urges. The day for progress by force has passed; it will be progress by ideas or not at all. And because these principles of free human cooperation between communities are, in a special sense, an English development, it is upon England that forms the responsibility of giving a lead.[6]

The real conflict, he concluded, was not between Germany and England, but between democracy and autocracy, socialism and individualism, and especially reaction and progress "however one's sociological sympathies may classify them." But that was surely the point, and Angell's sympathies were never for a moment in doubt. He took it as a given that his own country was the guarantor of the operation of free economic forces and that "the extension of the dominating principle of the British Empire to European society as a whole is the solution of the international problem which this book argues." *The Great Illusion,* in other words, was a liberal-imperialist manifesto directed at an informed German readership. It was not an economic text, merely concerned with free market principles.

But then again, all economic theories incorporate philosophies of how markets work, or should do, and how people behave, or rather should be encouraged to. Ideas matter, and the story of the outbreak of war in 1914 is that of the collapse of an entire system of thought – the progressive weakening of liberal thinking in Germany; the rise of a *zero-sum* competitive

---

[5] Peter Hopkirk, *On Secret Service east of Constantinople* (London: John Murray 2006), 25
[6] Niall Ferguson, *The Pity of War* (London: Allen Lane 1998), 6

idea of political economy, coupled with a profound disdain for economics itself. The enthusiasm with which Europe's youth went to war in 1914 was partly the manifestation of a collective boredom produced by the long peace.

The third problem with Angell's argument was that he put his trust in the fact that "lines of division on moral questions are within the nations themselves and intersect political frontier." Just as there was no modern state that was completely Catholic or Protestant, so he believed there was a strong liberal tradition in Germany, just as there was a strong protectionist tradition in the UK. And, of course, he was right. But the problem was that liberalism was not strong enough to make its voice heard over the forces of nationalism when the moment came. An overwhelming number of English liberals opposed to war may have stifled their misgivings in patriotic declarations when war broke out, but many prominent German Liberals such as Max Weber, Hans Delbruck, and Friedrich Neumann were not opposed to war itself. All three were resigned to the fact that a general European war was probably "inevitable."

Angell found this at first hand when he took his peace campaign to Germany itself in 1913. 2,000 copies of the German translation of *The Great Illusion* were distributed to a select group of German professors and students. Angell's German sponsors reckoned that even if many students would not attend his meetings – and few did – German universities would at least be exposed to his ideas. But both found the climate of opinion to be distinctly hostile. At the University of Göttingen, 25 students left the room as Angell began to speak in English and proceeded to the police station to complain that a political meeting was been held in a foreign language. In Berlin, the meeting ended in a fracas, with Angell complaining that some professors had goaded their students into heckling him.[7] Angell's tour had to be counted a failure. Germany was a nation whose youth were impatient to find a "place in the sun," even if the promise of that dream turned out to be the greatest illusion of all.

---

[7] Philip Supino, "The Norman Angell peace campaign in Germany," *Journal of Peace Research* 9/9 (1972), 164

Alternative Rationalities

"How little do we know our thoughts – our reflex actions, indeed, yes; but our reflex reflections?"

– Samuel Butler, The Way of all Flesh (1902)

In the title of Angell's book, *The Great Illusion,* the ghost of a better one lurked – our greatest illusion is our stubborn belief, all evidence to the contrary, in our ability to reason out what is best for us. Unfortunately, we don't always appreciate what is in our own best interests because we are not very rational or not as rational as we like to think. We are also chronically incapable of learning from experience or dealing with the recurring dilemmas of life. It is not a view, of course, which fits easily with the liberal worldview, and worldviews are anchored to ideas about life, which in turn condition the way we look at reality.

Angell won the Nobel Peace Prize in 1921. The following year's winner, the today little-known Norwegian historian Christian Lous Lange, extolled Angell's book in his own acceptance speech. What he found especially inspiring was "a profound and warm belief in what he calls in one of his books, 'the potential rationalism of mankind.'" Yet Angell's rationalism was largely devoid of human passion. Looking back on Europe's atavistic militarism, one of the most famous of 20th century liberals, Bertrand Russell, broke with convention by critiquing the extent to which his fellow liberals tended to over-emphasize human needs and consequently to ignore human desires. If impulse and desire were important, he insisted, so too was the desire for activity, which calls into play the need to excel; the sense of successfully overcoming resistance and the respect that success usually wins in the eyes of others.[8]

Russell himself was greatly influenced by the work of the American philosopher and psychologist William James, who had argued just before the war that military sentiments were too deeply grounded in human nature to be renounced until such time as better substitutes for national glory could be

---

[8] Bertrand Russell, *Why Men Fight* (London: Routledge 2010), 54

found than the returns of trade. The latter might well be the "best" avenue to plunder, but some societies aspired to achieve much more.

The importance of James's work is that he recognized that both the War Party and Peace Party were equally rational. Indeed, from the very beginning of his career (*A Sentiment of Rationality*, 1878) he had argued that rationality is itself merely a feeling or emotion. And James's work still appears in standard anthologies on logic because his argument, though not un-open to challenge, is actually quite persuasive. Some beliefs cannot be settled by intellect alone. James accepted that since beliefs harm others (and sometimes those who hold them), they should be as rational as they can, but he also insisted that they should also be life-affirming. He recognized that the arguments for war had to be met head-on and that the failure to do so was a failure of the liberal imagination, a failure on the part of writers like Angell to grasp that ideas such as Social Darwinism tapped into deeply-held human passions, and it was the passions, not the ideas, that were most important. James insisted that a belief is always connected with the satisfaction of desires as well as needs. For the English, war really didn't serve any interests (and very few needs). For the Germans, it served the need for greater respect; it was a palliative for a crippling sense of *resentment*. And it was from this premise that he concluded that all truth is *biographical*. Reality is real if it is true for you.

Reality, in short, is not unitary but multiple. There are many ways of looking at the world and understanding life. No reality is more fundamental, let alone more "real," than another. There are many worlds out there coexisting, sometimes uneasily. This is at one with the modern understanding that reality is mediated by language, by concepts and symbols and especially by metaphors. To insist that something is true, right or real, James insisted, we must always ask: true for whom? True ideas are those a society can validate and corroborate from its own historical experience. Whereas previous theorists had thought of truth as a property possessed of the truth-bearer, James regarded it as a historical process. "The truth of an idea is not a stagnant property inherent in it. Truth *happens* to an idea. It *becomes* true; it is *made* true by events. Its verity *is* in fact an event, a process: the process namely of its verifying itself."[9]

For James, ideas about reality also explain very different *styles of behavior*. Some of us are more fearful of failure than we are of achieving success and

---

[9] Dennis Ford, *The Search for Meaning: a short history* (Berkeley: UP of California 2007), 145

prefer to be cautious. We prefer to rely, therefore, on what reason gets us to reason out, and to fall back on the evidence that comes to hand. Others are more interested in finding the truth or meaning to existence rather than avoiding errors of judgment, and some will even be willing to take a leap of faith into the future (at some personal risk to themselves). In other words, some people are willing to take risks that others are not.

Take the example he gives in *The Will to Believe* of a man climbing a mountain who finds himself in danger, which he can only escape by making a great leap across the abyss. Have faith, he insisted, and you will find the nerve to accomplish the leap successfully. Doubt and mistrust your ability to make the leap and you will probably fall into the abyss. "Refuse to believe and you shall indeed be right, for you shall irretrievably perish. But believe, and again you shall be right, for you shall save yourself."[10] Beliefs are manifest in feelings.

We now know what James did not, even though he was noted at the time for being a respected psychologist as well as philosopher. Risk-avoidance isn't mediated in the thinking part of the brain, but largely in the emotional one. Feeling at risk and acting recklessly is a "feeling" too. Rational thinking has little to do with risk-avoidance. What *is* rational is the way that we often try to justify the risks once we have decided to take them by invoking logic, or to rationalize our decision-making after the fact. Mathematicians also tell us that because the human brain is unable to "compute" all the variables of our relationship with the world, we tend to take emotional shortcuts.[11] James's leap of faith is a good example.

To be in favor of war or against it in 1914 was much more complicated than deciding on the merits or not of protectionism. A good argument could indeed be made that another Great Power war would be irrational (no one would emerge victorious; modern war in privileging defense over offense would be long and attritional). But rationality cannot win an argument if the arguments for and against are equally weighty, or if the evidence is not especially conclusive either way. The French went to war thinking that *elan* and *cran* (guts) would be enough to win through. Many in Germany believed that the British would remain neutral and so allow them to concentrate on defeating Russia (they were wrong). The British pinned their hopes on Germany

---

[10] Ibid., 148
[11] Nassim Taleb, *Fooled by Randomness* (London: Penguin 2001), 38

intervening to prevent the Austrians from provoking another Balkan war (the greatest illusion of all).

That is the problem for all of us on a day-to-day basis. What do we choose to believe? What we have the *right* to believe is even more challenging if the matter exceeds our understanding. Most of us, in such matters, say of climate change or nuclear energy, rely on expert opinion, but experts are always at odds with each other. And anyway, a belief in global warming is influenced largely by scientific projections based on computer models; we have to take them on trust. And in France the military experts just happened to be convinced in 1914 of the power of the offensive against the defense, anchored to the unquestioning "logic" of national *elan*.

Now, of course – and this needs to be recognized at once – James's reasoning was itself biographical: it reflected the spirit of Pragmatism, the chief American contribution to philosophy, one that is still deeply entrenched in the way Americans still tend to view the world. James recognized that different societies have different cultural constructions of reality; the American happens to be consequentialist. [12] War is a given. Whether it is right or wrong (and James himself, as a pacifist, thought it was wrong), every society has to ask itself the question: what concrete difference will going to war make to my life? The meaning of war is to be found not in its origins but its consequences. In the end, the only decisive argument against going to war in 1914 was that Germany had an *unreasonable,* not irrational, hope of winning.

James was the forefather of what another contemporary American philosopher Charles Peirce called "fallibilism," our chronic inability to be rational. Other fallibilists include Karl Popper, who distrusted all intellectual certainty; Friedrich Hayek, who distrusted government certainty; Herbert Simon, who insisted that all rationality is "bounded"; and Daniel Kahneman and Amos Tversky, who argue that all our decisions are based on some often very irrational heuristics and biases. Even in science, the anti-positivists tell us that indeterminacy is the name of the game.

Bismarck was a fallibilist too, a highly intelligent man who appreciated how easy it us for us to believe what we want to. He tried, for that reason, to rein in German ambitions, but he was also an old man, a representative of a Europe that was already passing into history. The new Germany was

---

[12] Ford, The Search for Meaning: A short history, 148

reluctant to recognize constraints on its power and tired of Bismarck long before William II dismissed him. But one of the reasons for Bismarck's caution was his willingness to admit to something his successors wouldn't: Germany was actually a much weaker power than Britain or France, and defeat in war could well bring the whole edifice crumbling down. Even the prospect of victory worried him. As one diplomat wrote, Germany had had to pay for the victory of 1870 with universal suffrage. "Another victory will bring us a Parliamentary regime."[13] Success in war might unleash populist sentiments and ambitions that the state might not be able to contain.

It was not that Germany as a country was weak; its constitution was. The Parliamentary system, though based on universal suffrage, was rendered ineffective by the limitations placed on Parliament itself. Its most important power was control of the budget, but the military budget was only approved every five years, thus reducing its power of oversight. And though Parliament might express no confidence in the Chancellor, it could not remove him from office. Germany, in short, was a democracy of sorts, but an illiberal one. It was a vivid example of "reactionary modernism."

And when it came to the countdown to war, this proved fatal, as too did the concentration of the assessment of war plans and policy in one very inadequate person. Almost 50 men had direct access to the Emperor, but there were no routines to discuss or coordinate among or between them. Even information about the war plans was not shared between the General Staff, the War Ministry, the Admiralty, the Naval General Staff, or the Foreign Office. It was, writes John Keegan, as if sixty years later the US Strategic Air Command (SAC) had enjoyed the freedom to write plans for a nuclear war against the Soviet Union without reference to the Navy, the Army, or the State Department and as if the President had been left to circulate within his administration details of the war planning as he saw fit.[14]

So, one "lesson" to be learned from the First World War is that investing one's hope in war is not – from a cultural point of view – necessarily irrational at all; thinking you can win might well be. James was arguing that leaps in the dark, betting on luck, or trusting to providence were (and are) quite "rational." Irrationality came from knowing, or suspecting, the fatal consequences of taking such a leap and still going ahead. Take Field Marshall von Moltke, who advised the Kaiser in a secret memorandum that was only discovered in the

---

[13] Donald Kagan, *On the Origins of War* (London: Hutchinson 1995), 173
[14] Keegan, *The First World War* (London: Hutchinson 1998), 51

1980s that war would not be short (as the generals publicly claimed) but probably quite long and most likely end in the exhaustion of all the powers. Or take the German navy, which, having abandoned the arms race with Britain in 1912, perversely began preparing for a naval war at exactly the same time.[15]

At the outbreak of the war, the German Chancellor Bethmann-Hollweg was so pessimistic about the eventual outcome that he told his son there was no point in planting the family estate with new elm trees because the Russians would cut them down in thirty years' time (an accurate forecast, as it turned out; they did indeed arrive thirty years later and stayed for another fifty).[16] We all live with such conflicting ideas. Rational people live much of the time unreasonable lives.

Why the Rational Actor Model Doesn't Always Apply

We only think otherwise because American political science is in thrall to the rational actor model, which, in its canonical formulation, presumes that individuals make economic choices aimed at maximizing material payoffs based on all available information. The model is not wrong in presuming that – most of the time – we do indeed try to be rational; the problem is that we are not very intelligent. We have great difficulty identifying our true interests.

An especially telling example is the financial crisis of 2008, which could be explained by notable failures on the part of Alan Greenspan, the former Chairman of the Federal Reserve, including persuading the US Congress not to regulate the futures derivatives market. Later he admitted that he had been "shocked" to discover that financial houses and banks had not acted rationally in their own self-interest (in providing loans to people with no prospect of ever paying them back). It is an all too vivid example of what George Gilder calls "the incalculable subjectivity" of economists and the resulting impossibility of "calculable rationality" in human affairs.[17]

Even if we were more intelligent, social psychologists explain that our intelligence is strictly constrained. Back in the 1950s, writers such as Herbert Simon and a small group at the Harvard Business School begin to point out

---

[15] Donald Kagan, *On the Origins of War* (London: Hutchinson 1995), 148
[16] Norman Stone, *The First World War: A Short History* (London: Allen Lane 2007), 16
[17] George Gilder, *Wealth and Poverty* (New York: Basic Books 1981), 248

that our limited computational and predictive capabilities significantly constrain our ability to make utility-maximizing choices. The everyday problems we encounter in obtaining information and making the right calculations given the limited data available make it more than probable that our decisions will fall far short of the ideal of "maximizing" postulated by economic theory. The Nobel Prize-winning economist Daniel Kahneman is one exponent of *bounded rationality*; Simon, who was another Nobel Laureate in Economics, was the first to argue that organizations and people adopt principles of behavior that allow them to make acceptable, but not the best, decisions. One of the most important examples is "satisficing" (the melding of two words, satisfy and suffice). Unable to evaluate all outcomes with sufficient precision, we make do with the best alternative available. We stop when we get a near-satisfactory solution to a problem; if we did not choose to do so, it would take far too long to reach the smallest conclusion or perform the smallest act. We are therefore rational but only in a "bounded" way; it is the best we can do.[18] Economists tend to accept Simon but to reject Kahneman; they are willing, albeit grudgingly, to accept that we are flawed, but they are much less willing to acknowledge that we are imperfect machines: we are not very good at working out what is in our true interests.

Economists tend to believe that if governments don't run economies on rational lines, they ought to, so they often pretend that they do. They often oversimplify things, too, presenting the normal elements of any economy, such as strikes and corruption and tariffs, as aberrations. One of the fundamental problems with rational choice is that everything is forced to fit (every apparent anomaly or "odd" case), with the result that the case gets mangled or mutilated. And economists do all this in the name of "science" when economics is anything but scientific. A popular book that adopts this approach is *Predictably Irrational* (2008). But as John Kay writes, if people really are "predictably" irrational, then perhaps they are not really irrational at all. Perhaps the real fault lies not with the world but with our understanding of rationality.[19] We try to be rational, of course – we are in thrall to reason, but we are simply not very bright. Our "rational" decisions too often end disastrously for that reason. Many economists know this well enough – that is why they awarded Kahneman the Nobel Prize – but they have also

---

[18] Mahzarin Banaji, "Our Bonded Rationality" in John Brockman (ed), *This Explains Everything* (London: Harper 2013), 95

[19] John Kay, *Obliquity: why our goals are best achieved indirectly* (London: Profile 2011), xii

sidelined him because it has proved impossible to factor irrationality into their computer models; it is impossible to do the math.

The problem, unfortunately, is not confined to economics. As Donald Green and Ian Shapiro write, there is more to political behavior than just incentives and opportunities. Not all thought-systems are universal; culture actually matters. Rationality, as James insisted, is indeed biographical. Rational choice can't deal with biographical profiling because it is too complex. When analyzing political protests, for example, political scientists often prefer to ignore popular enthusiasm, attitudes towards leaders in a movement, feelings of personal inadequacy on the part of the protesters, or even the wish to participate in something larger than the individual self.[20] And if this is true of protest movements, it is also often true of war, which often breaks out not because decision-makers are ill-informed, but because they fall victim to cognitive dissonance or confirmation bias. In their book *War and Social Thought* (2012), the authors take issue with sociologists such as Charles Tilly and Michael Mann for rooting their models in rational action and not doing justice to social reality. They criticize them for taking insufficient note of societal processes that have unforeseeable and at times disastrous consequences and for failing to accept, on the evidence of history, that war can be provoked for its own sake.[21]

In other words, rational choice (to quote James) is unable to "plumb the thickness of reality." Economic models are unequal to the task of mapping actual human behavior. The things we often prize most are the things we won't exchange, the things that cannot be priced, such as reputation. Of course, unlike 1914, we can try to plumb reality in computer-modeling; we can program in vast amounts of data thanks to ever more sophisticated algorithms. But even in the case of pure logic rather than rationality, we still cannot design an error-free computer program. In principle, of course, a computer program should be as near as one gets to "pure thought" unsullied by day-to-day reality; unlike other media (such as wood, which splits, or paint, which smears), it is exceedingly tractable. In practice, errors arise all the time. Because so many programs can be written to perform the same function, they are really inevitable. And then there is the irreducible complexity of

---

[20] Evgeny Morozov, *To Save Everything, Click Here* (London: Allen Lane 2013), 41-42
[21] Joas/Knobel, War in Social Thought, 255

autonomously independent systems interacting with unpredictable inputs, which are often driven by even more unpredictable human actions.[22]

Our models make us honest, but they also make us complacent, too. They encourage us to believe that one size fits all; that what is true for us must be true for others. James insisted that many of the decisions we take in life are chosen by faith, not argument. Our beliefs are "adopted faiths" that we misconstrue as "logical." Cultural preferences, especially the "will to believe," or to take a bet on chance, James's leap of faith, are strongly reinforced by a sense of self. And if rationality is biographical, as he claimed, it probably counts for much that some societies feel they are owned more by history than others. A belief in a country's exceptionalism may even encourage risk-taking. Angell's contemporaries too, held to a pre-theoretical version of rational choice, only to find, to quote James, that all their versions of reality were only "a passionate affirmation of the desire in which our social system backs us up."[23] In other words, the thesis Angell put forward just happened to be true for him as a liberal and doubly true for him as an early twentieth century Englishman. Even so, in 1914 England, too, took a leap in the dark.

None of this gainsays other more material explanations for why war broke out in 1914, including the still widely held view that it was a consequence of several behavioral factors – political mistakes, uninformed anxieties, major misjudgments, and irrational drives. This is why behavioral economics continues to play such a central role in our understanding of it, with rational choice still taking center-stage. But I suspect that rationality itself holds the key – our perceptions of the world, our worldviews. A focus on rationality does not mean a reduced emphasis on behavior, just a richer understanding of it.

The Coming Sino-American War?

For me, the main take-away from 1914 is this. None of the Great Powers actually wanted war, but some were ready enough to seize the moment when it came. And they allowed the moment to escape control because no one really thought that the summer crisis occasioned by the Archduke Ferdinand's death would end in a European conflagration. The real

---

[22] Martin Hearst, 'Why Programs Have Bugs' in John Brockman (ed), *This Explains Everything* (New York: Harper Collins 2013), 226
[23] Ford, *The Search for Meaning*, 149

explanation, then, is the peculiar optimism that lulled the European political elite into a false sense of confidence that peace would hold come what might and the peculiar optimism that seized the Germans in particular that they could risk all in a war and still prevail.

Unfortunately, we are still telling ourselves the same story the statesmen did in 1913. One is the comforting view that globalization has made war even more unimaginable than it was then – national markets are even more interconnected; war between advanced economies would be "counter-productive either as a mechanism for resolving inter-state conflict or as a mechanism for transforming the international status-quo."[24] But this story is only as compelling as your belief in it – in some respects, the world was even more inter-dependent on the eve of the First World War than it is today. The point that needs emphasizing is that economic interdependence will not prevent war if a power concludes that it has a chance of success should the right circumstances present themselves; such a recourse to violence may be unreasonable but not necessarily irrational.

Perhaps if it comes to a choice, we will demand to be esteemed by others even at risk to our economic well-being. The German demand for respect was partly responsible for its diplomatic isolation and the same could be true of China. Indeed, one writer, Xie Tao (the author of *Living with the Dragon*), believes China is precisely on a collision course with the US because it is pursuing two incompatible objectives. "If you respect me, you won't challenge me; if you challenge me you clearly don't respect me" – the idea of earning respect by meeting another power halfway is becoming as difficult for the regime to grasp as it was for the Imperial German government. (*New York Times International*, 12 December 2013)

Unfortunately, we are placing far too many bets on rational choice. For at least two writers, the fundamental question is: should the US deal with Beijing with carrot and stick or just sticks? The answer is easy. America should not seek to democratize China but to make it what a Bush administration official in 2005 called "a responsible stakeholder" in the system. China can be "socialized." Reason dictates that it cannot be contained. Reason, the authors insist, must surely convince the Chinese that it will not be possible to replace American domination in East Asia with its own unilateral hegemony. And reason should dictate that Japan and Vietnam can be relied upon to

---

[24] David Held/Andrew McGrew, 'The End of the Old Order?', *Review of International Studies* 24 (1998), 222

oppose it themselves. But I doubt whether the Americans have any *reason* to trust the Chinese management of North Korea any more than the Europeans in 1913 could trust Germany's management of Austria-Hungary or Russia's management of Serbia.

Ultimately, our authors maintain, reason dictates that "the Americans and Chinese must recognize that no possible gains to either from a clash between them could compensate for the damage that such a clash would do to both of them."[25] Such a conflict would probably wreck America's capacity for global leadership, possibly for decades, and end China's hopes of emerging as a great power. But they are far too optimistic about the capacity of states to reason out their own best interests. The US palpably failed, as they themselves point out, in its own overreaction to 9/11. And there is no "reason" to suspect the Chinese of being any more sophisticated in reasoning out what is in their best interests anyway.

Another book that suggests that war is improbable is Noah Feldman's *Cool War, the Future of Global Competition* (2013). Both sides, he contends, have too much to lose. War would simply cripple the economies of both countries and in the case of China endanger Party rule. It would "simply be irrational" to go to war. But just because something is irrational does not mean it cannot happen. There are many examples in history of intelligent governments being right for the wrong reasons, and, when driven by their anxieties and demons, wrong for the wrong reasons. We are rarely right for the right reasons. There are plenty of flashpoints that could provoke a conflict (Taiwan, for one), and there are many real obstacles to cooperation, however open-minded the protagonists.

Feldman is probably right, at least on one point: in suggesting that American exceptionalism may prove a problem. If you are the Chinese leadership, it must be frustrating to have to sit down and negotiate policies with a government that thinks you are illegitimate because you are not democratically elected. It must be even more frustrating to know that your chief negotiating partner would actually like to see the end of your regime. This is not a good starting point, Feldman adds, for mutual trust or respect. I doubt, though, whether the US is going to change any time soon. The fact is that the two societies will find themselves on a collision course soon enough if neither can *earn* the trust and respect of the other.

---

[25] Anatol Lieven/John Hulsman, *Ethical Realism: a vision of America's role in the world* (New York: Pantheon 2006), 171

As Lee Kuan Yew remarked in 2013, "competition between the US and China is inevitable, but conflict is not."[26] It is a comforting thought and not one to be dismissed lightly, but wars are not always triggered by intelligent design, but by accidents, mishaps, and miscalculations as well as passions such as nationalism. War is unpredictable for that reason. Indeed, reason often has little to do with it.

Meanwhile, the clock is ticking. As the Japanese and Chinese once again drifted into another diplomatic spat as 2013 drew to a close, the US Vice President Joe Biden pronounced: China was at an "inflection point," a moment of dramatic change. It is a term that in mathematics (Wikipedia tells me) is used to describe how a curve shifts from convex to concave, or vice versa. It is probably pretty meaningless to use it in international affairs, but the real point was well-taken: the extraordinary economic growth of the past decade has made China increasingly overconfident at the same time that it is becoming resentful of its diplomatic isolation. The country has few friends. Commenting on Biden's remarks, Chinese professor Zhang Lifan remarked that the system in China would have to change if the country was to avoid a conflict with the US – the Party would have to become less paranoid and suspicious of the outside world and more amenable to change within; the society would have to become more open. The alternative, he added, was not desirable: China might want to reset the rules of the international system, as it had shown by its provocative behavior in the south China Seas (*New York Times International*, 12 December 2013). It is a sobering conclusion on a reading of history; for that is how most Great Power wars in the past three hundred years have begun.

---

[26] G Allison, "Interview with Lee Kwan Yew on the future of the US-China relations," *Atlantic* March 5 2013

Ernst Barlach, "Moses"

British soldiers eating at the Battle of the Somme, World War I

Make Concert, Not War: Power Change, Conflict Constellations, and the Chance to Avoid Another 1914

Harald Müller and Carsten Rauch

Abstract:

Do we have to worry about a new global confrontation a century after 1914? WWI happened amidst power shifts when European multipolarity rigidified into a confrontational two-alliance bipolarity. While there are some indicators that the same could happen again, there are also barriers today: The current power shift does not only concern Washington and Beijing, but rather two declining (US, Russia) and two rising (China, India) powers, and there are cross-cutting interests across potential Indian/US and Russian/Chinese alliance constellations. Building a new concert of powers, inspired by the pivotal security management tool of the 19th century that decayed on the eve of WWI, may help reduce the risks of great power conflict and manage a peaceful power transition.

A hundred years ago, the great powers went to war with each other. Whether they stumbled or sleepwalked into it[1] or World War I can be understood as a race for world power[2], the eve of the war was marked by two important trends: global shifts in power and a decay in the once-successful European Concert.

Current world politics display some similarities. World power is in flux and shifting among the great powers, which quarrel about issues like who owns Crimea or vast maritime areas in the South China Sea. Cloaked by the temporary (and still existing) dominance of the United States, growth rates of non-western economies like Brazil and India are significantly above those of established powers. China, with its spectacular double-digit rise for nearly two decades, might overtake the US in less than one generation. The center of world politics seems to be shifting to Asia – the US's "pivot" is indicative. World War I was (mostly) fought by European powers in Europe; control over

---
[1] Christopher Clark, *The Sleepwalkers: How Europe Went to War in 1914* (London: Penguin Books Ltd. 2012).
[2] Fritz Fischer, *Griff nach der Weltmacht: die Kriegszielpolitik des kaiserlichen Deutschland 1914/18* (Düsseldorf: Droste 1967).

the European system was the prize. Today both the most dynamic powers and the most troubling conflicts are located in Asia. Current multilateral (security) institutions appear insufficient to deal with these challenges.

As a possible solution to soothe the perils connected with these challenges, we propose a fresh look at the concert concept. The European Concert of the 19th century worked for a very long time during an era in which the right to war was part of sovereignty and more socially accepted than nowadays. It has demonstrated the possibility of bringing great powers together despite their divergent interests and cultural heritages and transform them into peace managers.[3] If it was possible to make Tsarist Russia, Victorian England, Republican France, militarist Prussia and Habsburgian Austria work for European stability, it is worth considering whether a similar arrangement might be able to maintain global stability today.

In the following article, we first outline the concept of power transition and highlight the differences in the power shifts in the early twentieth and early twenty-first centuries. We then discuss the conflict dynamics that paved the way for World War I and sketch similarities and differences between today and 1914. After that, we develop several escalation scenarios before turning to the question of which existing or at least imaginable management tools were/are available to defuse the risks of a contemporary great power war. We conclude by pointing out the deficiencies in the security institutions of 1914 and today and highlighting the prospects of a modernized concert of powers that may present the world's best chance to prevent a fatal repetition of history.

Power Transitions: Ideal Type, 1914 and Today

The power transition allegory is often evoked when the consequences of ongoing global power shifts are discussed. Power transition theory (PTT) is a tool for those who forecast conflict between a rising China and a declining

---

[3] Matthias Schulz, Normen und Praxis - Das europäische Konzert der Großmächte als Sicherheitsrat, 1815 - 1860 (München: Oldenbourg 2009); Harald Müller and Carsten Rauch, Managing Power Transition with a "Concert of Powers"?, Paper prepared for presentation at the ISA Annual Convention 2011: March 16-19 (Montreal 2011); Harald Müller and Carsten Rauch, „Machtübergangsmanagment durch ein Mächtekonzert. Plädoyer für ein neues Instrument zur multilateralen Sicherheitskooperation," Zeitschrift für Friedens- und Konfliktforschung (forthcoming 2015).

US. The picture becomes a little blurrier, however, when one takes PTT's assumptions seriously.

Massive power disruptions characterized the pre-1914 period just as they characterize today's. However, not every power shift is a power *transition*. Power transitions take place at the top of the international order, when a challenger overtakes the former dominant power. According to PTT, power transition mechanisms become relevant even earlier, when a challenger approaches parity (commonly 80% of the hegemon's power resources). Parity opens a window of opportunity in which both parties can sensibly hope for victory in war.

PTT was originally conceived by A.F.K. Organski[4]; later, Organski, Jacek Kugler, and numerous other authors developed a power transition research program.[5] It rests on the assumption that the international system resembles a hierarchy much more than the realist-inspired anarchy, and thus becomes an international order. At the top of the international power pyramid, the strongest power, the hegemon, dominates the international system. This dominant power once established the international order (often following a major war) according to its interests, desires, and normative beliefs and guards it against would-be challengers. As this order is typically geared towards producing benefits primarily for the dominant power and its allies, PTT generally expects non-privileged actors to be dissatisfied. These powers have an intrinsic motivation and a willingness to change the status quo. Most dissatisfied powers are small or middle powers and can thus be neglected by the dominant power. However, the situation turns dangerous when a great power becomes dissatisfied or when a dissatisfied power starts to rise. When the challenger closes the gap to the dominant power, an opportunity opens: Since the dominant power is not strong enough anymore to safely ensure victory in war, a dissatisfied rising power may be tempted to change the international order by force. When opportunity and willingness converge, PTT sees war as a serious possibility. PTT, however, is not deterministic. A

---

[4] A.F.K. Organski, *World Politics* (New York, NY: Knopf 1958).
[5] See: A.F.K. Organski and Jacek Kugler, *The War Ledger* (Chicago et al.: University of Chicago Press 1980); Jacek Kugler and Douglas Lemke (eds), *Parity and War - Evaluations and Extensions of the War Ledger* (Ann Arbor, MI: University of Michigan Press 1996); Ronald L. Tammen, Jacek Kugler, Douglas Lemke, Allan C. Stamm, III, Mark Abdollahian, Carole Alsharabati, Brian Efrid and A. F.K. Organski, *Power Transitions: Strategies for the 21st Century* (New York, NY: Seven Bridges Press 2000).

peaceful power transition is consistent with the theory if the rising power is not dissatisfied with the international order.⁶

Figure 1: The Power Relation between the UK and the US 1850-1900

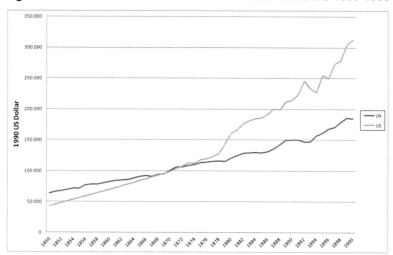

---

⁶ Carsten Rauch, Das Konzept des friedlichen Machtübergangs: Die Machtübergangstheorie und der weltpolitische Aufstieg Indiens (Baden-Baden: Nomos 2014).

Figure 2: The Power Relation between the UK and Germany 1870-1914

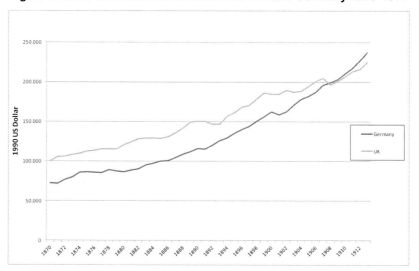

While the 19th century in general witnessed rather glacial power developments, there were two exceptions (see Figures 1 and 2). Great Britain had averted the challenge of revolutionary and Napoleonic France and remained dominant since. According to GDP figures[7], the United States overtook Great Britain in 1869, but since the US was not entangled in Europe, then the center of the international system, PTT scholars tend to ignore this transition.[8] In the late 19th century, after German unification, Berlin began to close the gap with London.[9] Germany reached parity in 1895 and overtook Britain in 1908. In 1914 Germany was in the lead but both powers were still in a zone of parity. At the same time, German leaders were worried about the rise of Russia and the prospect of another power transition.

---

[7] All historical GDP figures are taken from Angus Maddison, "Historical Statistics of the World Economy: 1-2006 AD,"
<http://www.ggdc.net/maddison/Historical_Statistics/horizontal-file_02-2010.xls>.

[8] Some scholars count it as peaceful power transition; a recent account calls it an "overslept" power transition. See: Feng Yongpin, "The Peaceful Transition of Power from the UK to the US," *Chinese Journal of International Politics* 1/1 (2006); Rauch, *Konzept*, 170.

[9] Paul M. Kennedy, *The Rise and Fall of the Great Powers-Economic Change and Military Conflict from 1500 to 2000* (New York, NY: Random House 1987); Volker Ullrich, *Die nervöse Grossmacht - Aufstieg und Untergang des deutschen Kaiserreichs 1871 - 1918* (Frankfurt am Main: Fischer 1997).

The United States consciously adopted the role of dominant power after the end of World War II. The Soviet Union, challenger throughout the Cold War, never came close to reaching parity. The rising powers of today, notably China, have much higher growth rates than the United States, but the US is still far ahead in total numbers. As of 2012[10], China's GDP is about 51% of the US's, at some distance from parity (see Figure 3).[11]

Figure 3: The Power Relation of the United States and China 1960-2012

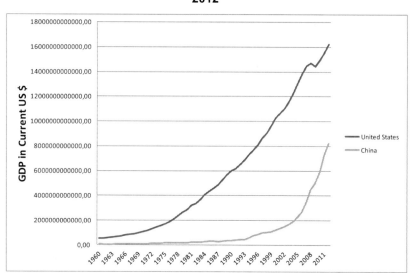

Shifting the focus from GDP totals to growth rates, the US, the EU, Russia, and Japan are in *relative* decline. China, India, Brazil and other rising powers are growing much faster. This trend has been going on for two decades. In the long run, a power transition seems possible. It will be a power transition of a new type. While PTT is typically dyadic (one dominant power vs. one rising power), the current situation is complex. Several powers are rising and growing faster than the US. At the moment Beijing has apparently the best chance to overtake Washington and become the new dominant power. But

---

[10] All contemporary GDP figures are taken from the World Bank <http://data.worldbank.org/indicator/NY.GDP.MKTP.CD>.

[11] Other rising powers fare worse: in 2012, Brazil reached about 14% of the US's GDP and India just 11%.

the existence of multiple potential challengers creates the opportunity for springboard conflicts: before concentrating on the dominant power, different rising powers might compete for the best starting position. Further, the US's still-healthy margin provides time for managing the coming transition.

Power parity, however, is not a sufficient condition for a great power war. Other crucial factors include the rising power's satisfaction with status quo in the international order, its will to power, and overall great power relations.[12] The situation is most dangerous when a hegemon confronts a dissatisfied and power-hungry challenger and great power relations are generally antagonistic. Thus, for comparing 1914 with 2014, it is necessary to analyze contexts and power constellations.

World War I: Conflict Dynamics and Great Power Constellations

Scholarship on the causes of World War I in the past decades has moved towards complex rather than simple explanations. To blame a single party has lost traction in the last twenty years, despite a gallant effort by Fritz Fischer, Immanuel Geiss, John Röhl, and others to bolster the Versailles Treaty version of exclusive German guilt with scholarly evidence.[13] Most relevant newer studies distribute responsibility more equally across the major powers without denying the share accrued by the German Reich and Austria-Hungary.[14] In the following section, we discuss the elements of complex explanations in order to obtain a template against which to assess current dangers.

---

[12] Rauch, *Konzept*, Chapter 5.
[13] Fischer, Griff; Imanuel Geiss, *Der lange Weg in die Katastrophe: Die Vorgeschichte des Ersten Weltkriegs; 1815 - 1914* (München et al.: Piper 1990); Röhl, John C. G., *From Bismarck to Hitler: The problem of continuity in German history* (London: Longman 1970).
[14] Samuel R. Williamson, Jr., "July 1914 revisited and revised: the erosion of the German paradigm," in Jack S. Levy and John A. Vasquez (eds), *The outbreak of the First World War: Structure, politics, and decision-making* (Cambridge: Cambridge University Press 2014).

The Powers: Interests, Conflicts and Intentions

In the category of interests, the crucial category is revisionism. We distinguish between territorial and symbolic revisionism. Serbia (Bosnia-Herzegovina, Voivodina), France (Alsace-Lorraine), and Russia (control of the entry straits of the Black Sea) had interests to change the European landscape. Britain, Germany, and Austria-Hungary (after having annexed Bosnia-Herzegovina) were *territorially* rather satisfied and desired no further territorial expansion in Europe.

Symbolic revisionism is related to a desired change of status. Here, Germany was the most virulent case, desiring equality with Britain as a world power, expressed in the stubborn insistence on a colonial empire, and in the will to become a sea power. The latter ambition led Germany into a naval arms race with Britain in the first decade of the 20th century. Germany lost and Britain was driven into alliances with France and Russia and developed a deep distrust of the Reich. This distrust strengthened the anti-German group in the Foreign Office. On the eve of WWI, the naval arms race subsided as Germany conceded defeat, and relations seemed to improve, but the damage of pushing Britain into a fixed alliance was done.[15]

Great Britain and Austria-Hungary were status quo powers. Britain wanted to keep its place at the top and preserve a balance of power on the continent. British concerns for the Empire led the leadership to seek accommodation with France and Russia, the two powers that could endanger the British position in the colonies. The interest in appeasing Moscow and Paris inclined Britain to be more lenient towards their revisionism than its role as a "balancer" could bear. Austria-Hungary's political elite feared for the survival of the multi-ethnical empire under the pressures of Russia, revisionist and aggressive Serbia, Romania, and the virulent nationalism among its own minorities. This fear for its world power status and for the existence of the Double Monarchy motivated Austria-Hungary to use the best opportunity to fight a decisive war against the Serbian challenge.[16]

---

[15] Volker R. Berghahn and Wilhelm Deist, *Rüstung im Zeichen der wilhelminischen Weltpolitik: Grundlegende Dokumente 1890 - 1914* (Düsseldorf: Droste 1988), Lena Jaschob, "Status, Recognition and Global Political Dreams. The German Kaiserreich and its Naval Programme before World War I," Paper prepared for the 55th International Studies Association Convention, March 26th - 29th (Toronto 2014).

[16] On interests, cf. Karen Rasler and William R. Thompson, "Strategic rivalries and complex causality in 1914," in Jack S. Levy and John A. Vasquez (eds), The outbreak

Besides great powers, "spoilers" were present that were able to fuel conflicts and set in motion a chain of events leading to hostilities. Serbia is a case in point. Belgrade could not hope to achieve more than pinholes against Austria-Hungary without outside assistance, but its actions provoked Austrian hostilities and military action by Russia ensued.

Enemy Images, Fears, and Perceived Preemptive Needs

Governments on all sides were deeply distrustful of both partners and rivals. Austria-Hungary feared German defection and needed full-scale reassurance at all times. Both Vienna and Berlin believed that Russia was poised to eliminate the Double Monarchy as a great power. Germany thought that France was determined to reconquer Alsace-Lorraine, and that Great Britain was set to deny Berlin its well-deserved "place in the sun." That this place in the sun was a somewhat elusive concept, based less on concrete negotiable demands than on – among other things – the feeling of not getting proper recognition as a world power did not make it easier to accommodate the Reich even if London had wanted to do so. Britain in turn thought Germany to be profoundly revisionist and intent on imposing itself on all of Europe, while the French feared that Germany wanted to complete the reduction of French power status begun in 1871. All sides imputed the worst possible intentions on the others. This made it difficult to reverse course once the Sarajevo murders pushed intra-European tensions beyond the 'normal' threshold of previous crises.

The extreme fears of pre-emption must be added. There was a lingering feeling that war was inevitable sooner or later, mixed up with the deceptive optimism that it would not come tomorrow. The fear that one could be caught on the wrong foot was a combination of all these factors: If war would come, it was essential to take the initiative and not to wait for the enemy to mount a successful offensive. While this fear misread the character of the coming war, it had sunk deeply into the minds of military leaders and prevented all thought of reversing course once mobilization had started.[17]

---

    of the First World War: Structure, politics, and decision-making (Cambridge: Cambridge University Press 2014); Clark, Sleepwalkers, Chapters 3 and 5.

[17] Stephen van Evera, "The Cult of the Offensive and the Origins of the First World War," in Steven E. Miller, Sean M. Lynn-Jones and Stephen van Evera (eds), *Military strategy*

Doctrines

Military leaders believed in the superiority of the offensive. Germany was wedded to the "Schlieffen Plan," the right-wing sweep around French defenses that would envelop the whole French army, necessitating the violation of Belgian neutrality (and thereby bringing Britain into the war). France had long bet on a strategic defense but then switched to "Plan 17," a head-on offensive at the right and middle front sectors. Russia had promised the French ally that it would attack westwards in order to bind German forces in the East as early as possible, while Austria knew it had to face a Russian offensive while pressing its own attack against Serbia. The British expeditionary force would have to join the French offensive by default. Apart from war plans as such, the offensive orientation reflected deep beliefs about the balance between offensive and defensive, the value of the offensive for the spirit of the troops and the unity of the nation, and the dim prospects of a long, drawn-out war, which all continental powers had reasons to fear. In addition, the offensive fit the social Darwinist ideology, as one's own "genetic" superiority would show in the steely push forward that a military offensive would entail.[18]

Arms Races

The years preceding the war witnessed increasingly antagonistic interaction in the field of armaments. Political crises, underlined by military moves, stimulated further armament efforts: The two crises over Morocco, the Bosnia annexation crisis of 1908, the Libyan crisis provoked by the Italian offensive, and the two Balkan wars following the Italian assault on the Ottoman Empire's African position kept European diplomats busy and drove Austria to increasing panic. Every crisis led to reconsideration of each power's posture, focusing the military's, and increasingly the political leadership's attention on the perceived weaknesses of one's own position. France felt compelled to extend military service from two to three years. Germany enhanced the

---

    and the origins of the First World War. Revised and Expanded Version (Princeton, NJ: Princeton University Press 1991); Jack Snyder, *Myths of empire - domestic politics and international ambition*, Cornell studies in security affairs (Ithaca et. al: Cornell University Press 1991).

[18] van Evera, "Cult"; Snyder, *Myths*.

fighting strength of its troops and reinforced field artillery, achieving a significant advantage at the war's outset. Russia undertook a huge investment (with French credits) in railways to accelerate troop movements to its Western borders, the fundamental condition to support France by binding German forces in the East. Great Britain dived into ever more intense staff collaboration with France and enhanced its expedition force for a continental engagement. Austria strove to keep pace with the growth of Serbian, Montenegrin, and Romanian forces, which profited from French credits and arms supplies. Apart from the preparations on land, the naval arms race also continued.[19]

Maybe the most critical factor was the universal tendency to accelerate the speed of mobilization and deployment. The fear raged not to be able to withstand the first enemy assault: One day could be decisive. This race reflected, and reinforced, the belief that being even hours too late might be fatal for the nation's survival. These anxieties and the plans for mobilization, deployment, and marching forward that they had inspired, locked the antagonists into a sequence of actions that looked irreversible to the actors once it had started. The decisive factor was ultimately the Schlieffen Plan, which eliminated all flexibility from the system. Had Germany kept open the option of a defensive stance in the West and delivering battle in the East, history might have taken a different course, as Britain might have stayed out of the war.[20]

---

[19] David Stevenson, *Armaments and the coming of war: Europe, 1904 - 1914* (Oxford: Clarendon Press 1996).

[20] Richard N. Lebow, *A Cultural Theory of International Relations* (Cambridge et al.: Cambridge University Press 2008), 355–9. That, eventually, the Russian opening offensive was crushed at Tannenberg was a bitter irony because it vindicated the alternative option.

Today's Conflict Dynamics and Great Power Constellations

The Powers: Interests, Conflicts, and Intentions

War and peace in the 21st century will largely depend on the relationships among four powers: the United States, China, Russia, and India. They are entangled in a complex of overlapping disputes concerning themselves, allies, friends, and a related arms race including the nuclear dimension.

The US will remain the military hegemon for a while. American political elites will continue to see themselves the leaders of the world. Their main orientation is status quo, but powers defending their leadership position can turn revisionist, as the attempt to reshape the Middle East through force during the second Bush era has shown.

China provides the main challenge to US leadership. With its memory of a long history as the "middle kingdom" as well as of a dark century of humiliation at the hands of the West and Japan, the world's strongest-growing economy has given the Communist leadership new self-confidence. This assertiveness is combined with the desire for recognition emerging from a minority complex rooted in its "century of inferiority," and resentment against what China perceives as arrogance and discrimination displayed by Washington.[21] Chinese territorial demands betray a revisionist agenda, which in the Chinese mind appears as a restorative agenda, dedicated to bring back home lost territories on land and sea to which China has a just historical claim.

Russia's vast territory borders most of the world's important and/or conflict-loaded regions. This alone makes Russia a significant player, even though its power has declined since the high days of the Soviet Union. Its position as an energy producer continues to be a power asset, but the blunt way in which Putin has handled this asset leads to counter-measures that undercut Russian leverage. Its nuclear arsenal is another factor to be reckoned with. Russia's political elite harbors resentment against the West, particularly the US, dreams of the glorious days of the Soviet Union and pursues a revisionist agenda, as in the Georgian and Ukrainian crises.

---

[21] Yao Yunzhu, "China's Perspective on Nuclear Deterrence," *Air and Space Power Journal* 24/1 (2010).

The weakest, but rising, actor in the quartet is India. The Indian orientation is defensive, as India wants to maintain the territory it currently occupies (see below). Its elite is attached to symbolic revisionism, the strive for recognition as equal among the major powers, but it is not pursued with the same vigor as China. India maintains good relations with both the US and Russia and receives sufficient recognition from these powers to feel comfortable. Nevertheless, India seeks a greater role in world politics and shows a growing naval presence.

Additionally, there are a number of potential "spoilers" where not necessarily power but rather politics and location potentially enable governments to exert a disproportionate influence on the course of events. Japan, located in the crucial and crisis-prone East Asian region, is relevant not only because of its leading economic role and its remarkable but frequently overlooked military strength. Its alliance with the US defines to a certain degree the regional position of Japan towards China. Japanese nationalist revisionism (currently exemplified by Prime Minister Abe's revisionist desire to eliminate the constitutional curbs on military operations, which is supported by an assertive portion of both political elite and population), long overshadowed by Japan's apparent pacifism, has come to the fore in recent years and negatively impacts relations with China and South Korea. The nationalist factor in Japan is one of the potential "spoilers" that could drive the region into crisis. Pakistan is capable of exacerbating Indian-Chinese tensions and plays a key role for the Indian view on China through the support China affords to India's revisionist Western neighbor, which still harbors ambitions for Kashmir. That Pakistan must also be calculated into the nuclear equation makes this potential even more virulent. The same applies to North Korea, which has proven its readiness to produce artificial militarized crises many times, and whose incalculability and bizarre strategic calculus might be explosive when a situation is already tense. Strangely, Taiwan, though a blossoming and economically successful democracy, falls in the same category, as a possible drift towards independence might easily stir up Chinese brinkmanship. As smooth as the relations to the mainland are presently, a more independence-minded leadership – available in the current opposition party – can quickly cause a dangerous deterioration involving the United States.

China and the United States have no direct conflict with each other, yet their relationship contains the highest risk of all dyads in the quartet.[22] Their disputes arise from the US's role as formal (Japan, South Korea, Philippines) or informal (India, Taiwan, Vietnam) ally to states with which China has serious (territorial) quarrels[23] and from the rivalry for the top status position. The "pivot to Asia" reflects the seriousness of American commitment.[24]

In addition to the Pakistani issue and India's hosting the Dalai Lama, a bête noire for China, territorial issues divide China and India as well[25]: Aksai Chin, a strip of Kashmiri territory held by China but claimed by India, and the Indian state of Arunachal Pradesh (which the Chinese call South Tibet) of which China claims the northern part. A commission has been working on the issue for years without results, and occasional border incidents point to risks involved. It appears that India prefers legalizing the status quo, but this position does not yet resonate with Beijing.

Between Russia and the US, a declining security cooperation is increasingly overshadowed by geostrategic competition and a resuming arms race. Russian elites are upset by what they perceive as Washington having taken advantage of Russian weakness in the nineties rather than developing a true partnership. Eastern Europe, the Caucasus, and Central Asia are loci of struggles for influence. Where the attraction works strongly in the American direction as in Georgia or Ukraine, Moscow uses military action to assert its own weight. At least, Russia and the US have no quarrels in the hotbed of East/Southeast Asia. On the ideological front, the US despises Putin's parallel pursuit of autocratic governance and tongue-in-cheek claims of democratic rule and lawful external behavior. Fundamental differences on the Responsibility to Protect emerged in places like Sudan, Libya, or Syria, and geopolitical games played their role in Syria, Central Asia, the Caucasus, Eastern Europe, and Iran, a fact that did not prevent occasional cooperation such as on certain sanctions against Tehran or dismantlement of Syria's chemical weapons capabilities.

---

[22] Rosemary Foot and Andrew Walter, *China, the United States, and global order*, 1st publ. (Cambridge et al.: Cambridge University Press 2011).

[23] Bruce A. Elleman, Stephen Kotkin and Clive H. Schofield (eds), *Beijing's power and China's borders: Twenty neighbors in Asia* (Armonk, N.Y: M.E. Sharpe 2012).

[24] On the risks of an assertive US policy in this region, see: Hugh White, *The China choice: Why America should share power* (Collingwood, Vic: Black Inc. 2012).

[25] George J. Gilboy and Eric Heginbotham, *Chinese and Indian strategic behavior: Growing power and alarm* (Cambridge et al.: Cambridge University Press 2012).

The Russian-Chinese relationship has become very much a function of the US-Russian one. Conducted under the label of strategic partnership, it is a mixture of common interest against Washington's hegemony and military preponderance, traditional distrust, regional competition, and uncertainties about Chinese immigration in Eastern Siberia. The more tense the relations between the US and Russia and China, respectively, the closer the strategic relationship between the two autocracies is likely to develop.

Russia has retained the Soviet Union's smooth relations with India. In contrast, US attitudes towards New Delhi have undergone major changes since the Cold War. Unkind during the rivalry with the Soviet Union, Washington has warmed up to the rising Asian state since the mid-nineties, and offered a kind of security partnership, if not a true entente, under George W. Bush, hoping to use India as a counterweight against China.

Arms races, doctrines, and pre-emption

Political conflict and ensuing tensions reinforce the security dilemma and motivate precautionary measures to ensure one's capability for (self-)defense. In the US's case, the doctrine of superiority established in the 1990s still holds. In Russia's and increasingly China's cases, the desire to project power beyond one's borders in regions of interest translates into armament projects beyond pure self-defense. In all cases, the determination to establish or maintain a significant naval presence adds to armament dynamics.

The most virulent arms dynamics concern the land-sea-air-competition between the US and China. It circles around the US's effort to preserve its capability to defend Taiwan against a Chinese conquest and China striving to move towards sea denial for the US and, in the longer term, sea control in the Taiwan Strait and adjacent waters (anti-access/area denial (A2/AD)). The Chinese development of a mid-range missile arsenal (the DF-21D) to take out US aircraft carriers before they enter the zone of impact and Beijing's procurement of aircraft carriers creates potential sea control capabilities but also establishes a long-range maritime power projection option.[26] The US's *AirSea Battle* strategy wants to assert the Navy's penetration power in order

---

[26] Christian Le Mière, *Anti-access/Area denial and the South China Sea*, Paper presented at the Fourth International South China Sea Workshop, 19-21 November, Ho Chi Minh City, Vietnam (Ho Chi Minh City, Vietnam 2012).

to maintain sea control close to Chinese shores and aims at options to preempt China's mid-range strike assets; this objective necessitates deep penetration into the mainland. In addition, Chinese anti-satellite options, US defensive or preemptive options to counter them, and the invisible but apparently ambitious efforts on both sides to create offensive and defensive cyberwar potentials adds to the uncertainties engendered by this race.

Chinese-Indian military competition has a smaller land and a larger sea part to it. The Indians complain about Chinese reinforcements along the common border and take countermeasures. World War I experts will feel déjà vu reading about Indian concerns regarding the construction of the trans-Tibet railway which permits bringing Chinese troops much more rapidly to contested areas. The competition at sea involves the systematic enlargement of both navies and the Indian attempt to counter the "string of pearls," a series of anchoring possibilities and/or port facilities available to the Chinese navy in Burma, Bangladesh, Sri Lanka, and Pakistan. India has responded with its joint headquarters on the Andaman Islands, which control access to the Malacca Strait as well as access to the Bay of Bengals with its Chinese naval stations. In addition, India cultivates naval relations, including joint exercises, with Vietnam, the US, Australia, and Japan.[27]

The conventional US-Russian race has been decided in America's favor. Russia's recent attempts to improve the capabilities of its conventional forces appear to aim to create options against its smaller neighbors. However, there is an arms race in the nuclear realm between Russia and China on the one hand and the United States on the other.[28] This race is complicated because the moves of the two autocracies are meant to counter not only a US nuclear threat but to ensure the survivability of their deterrents against US long-range conventional options ("Prompt Global Strike") and against future US national missile defense.[29] Russia keeps a four-digit number of sub-strategic nuclear weapons to compensate for conventional inferiority. India is connected to this race by orientating its nuclear arms buildup towards countering China's slowly growing deterrent. Pakistan, the potential spoiler, views its nuclear

---

[27] T. Nirmala Devi and A. Subramanyam Raju, *India and Southeast Asia: Strategic convergence in the twenty-first century* (New Delhi: Manohar Publishers & Distributors 2012).

[28] Stephen J. Cimbala, *Arms for uncertainty: Nuclear weapons in US and Russian security policy* (Farnham: Ashgate 2013).

[29] Thomas Fingar, "Worrying about Washington: China's Views on the US Nuclear Posture," *The Nonproliferation Review* 18/1 (2011).

arsenal as a counter-deterrent to India's as well as a compensation for conventional inferiority.

The core issue connecting the conventional and the nuclear races starts from the American extended deterrence role in Asia.[30] The US wants to keep its nuclear arsenal credible for this function. At the same time, it is concerned that the growing invulnerability of the Chinese deterrent might encourage China to challenge this guarantee. The most disquieting feature in the military equation concerns the preemptive assumptions that are visible in the US-Chinese competition for prevailing in a (presently unlikely) Taiwan crisis. Two interconnected preemptive plans for the start of a military conflict constitute the most unstable nightmare one can dream up, and a disturbing analogy to the "cult of the offensive" prevailing at the outset of World War I among the major continental powers. The loser in the preemption race might then consider nuclear escalation.

Ideologies

There is no overarching ideology today like Social Darwinism before and during World War I. Nevertheless, ideology plays its role: The West, most pronouncedly the United States, is deeply averse to the non-liberal, non-democratic systems of rule in China and Russia. It ascribes to these regimes an inherent aggressiveness and wants to challenge their system of rule. America's allies share these preferences with differing degrees of enthusiasm and intensity, and many do not display the same degree of confrontational will that the US is occasionally ready to embrace.[31] The two challenged parties stick to an orthodox understanding of their sovereignty, which many in the West see as obsolete, and resent what they regard as undue interference in their internal affairs. They ascribe to American policy a long-term geostrategic plan to contain and subdue them, and then translate this view of the current world into their own geostrategic and geo-economic machinations. Their own ideological position is thus rather defensive and

---

[30] Andrew O'Neil, *Asia, the US and extended nuclear deterrence: Atomic umbrellas in the twenty-first century* (London, New York: Routledge, Taylor & Francis Group 2013).

[31] Anna Geis, Harald Müller, and Niklas Schörnig, "Liberal democracies as militant 'forces for the good': a comparative perspective," in Anna Geis, Harald Müller, and Niklas Schönig (eds), *The militant face of democracy: Liberal forces for good* (Cambridge: Cambridge University Press 2013).

reactive, but the effects look at times quite offensive and active (as China's naval showings in Asian seas or the Russian moves against Ukraine).

2014 is not 1914, but...

At first glance, the similarities between the constellations of 1914 and today are astounding. Today we find as many (if not more) revisionist powers. Arms dynamics are – again – visible most notably between the dominant and the primary rising power and, (nuclear) deterrence notwithstanding, offensive and preemptive military postures and assumptions – again – play an important role. Furthermore, the chasm between democracies and non-democracies has created a new conflict dimension (though Social Darwinism has luckily decreased in importance). These similarities should not be exaggerated, however. For example, and somewhat reassuringly, the world is not divided in two antagonistic power blocs that – fueled by the idea of Social Darwinism – are hell-bent to prove their respective superiority. Instead of a big conflict line around which all the deciding actors flock to one side or the other in rigid alliances, we rather have to deal with a number of more or less confrontational bilateral relationships that in turn have an impact on each other. One can also take comfort in the fact that among the six combinations of the four most important actors today, two do not seem to be troubling at all. On the other hand, it is troubling that all dyads, including the primary rising power, China, can be regarded as conflict-ridden. Regarding the other similarities, it should be noted that, while we find many dissatisfied powers today, their revisionism is probably somewhat muted compared to the aims of their 1914 counterparts. The same holds true for questions of armament and doctrines: Even though we cannot ignore the armament dynamic and offensive military postures of the powers today, the arms race situation was more severe in 1914 and the cult of the offensive more pronounced. However, while the powder-keg of today may be a little less unstable than the one in 1914, it still remains a powder-keg in need of defusing. In the next section, we present two escalation scenarios demonstrating this need.

Escalation Scenarios

The dangerous characteristic of an interconnected conflict complex is that a crisis in one of its components possesses the capability to trigger ripple effects throughout the whole system. July/August 1914 was a case in point. The Ukrainian crisis in March 2014 shows that the Asian conflict complex has not yet achieved full interconnectedness. Russia is a great power, and is also present, though peripherally, in East Asia. Nevertheless, the Ukrainian events have not yet had lasting repercussions in the Asian region. Despite a few top level encounters and the signing of several agreements between Moscow and Beijing, China demonstrated its neutrality by abstaining on the UNSC draft resolution calling for the condemnation of Russia. However, the crisis may engender the consequence of strengthening interconnectedness politically: After Russia positioned itself squarely against the West, Western powers reacted with sanctions that are likely to further deepen the rift. It is quite likely that Russia will seek compensation by leaning more strongly towards China. It cannot be ruled out that military cooperation between the two powers in Eastern Asia may visibly rise in the next years; the unprecedented military exercises that Russia and China held in August 2014 in inner Mongolia in the framework of the Shanghai Cooperation Organization (Kazakhstan, Kyrgyzstan, and Tajikistan also participated) thus might be a forerunner of things to come.

Even among the various theaters making up the Asian conflict complex, interconnectedness is not yet complete. The militarized dispute between China and Japan concerning the Senkaku/Diaoyu Islands was not accompanied by rising tensions either in the Taiwan Strait (on the Diaoyu Islands, the People's Republic and Taiwan take very similar positions) or in the South China Sea or the Himalaya and Karakorum. As long as this divisibility of theaters remains, a violent conflict in one of the theaters might be locally contained and managed. However, even under these circumstances, the caveat has to be recognized that divisibility might fall by the wayside once a conflict involves China and the USA from the outset. China's multiple conflicts with the most powerful state and a couple of its allies may well lead to classical overextension; but the same prospect 100 years ago did not prevent Germany from entering a multi-front war.

In what follows, two scenarios are drawn, neither of which is completely improbable, each of which requires a sequence of things going wrong (which is not preordained), and each of which depends on a series of priority-setting decisions on either side of the aisle that set the course in the direction of war. In that, the scenarios do not deviate from historical precedence in one direction or the other. In the Cuban missile crisis, several things happened that worsened the situation and paved the road for other things that could happen to further worsen it. These sequential things, however, did not happen, and the superpowers extracted themselves from a "nuclear Sarajevo." In July 1914, bad things happened that paved the road for worse things to come, and these worse things did indeed happen, with fatal consequences.

Scenario I. Simply Taiwan

Let us imagine that future US-Chinese relations will suffer higher tensions than today, but no direct deadly conflicts. In their distinct roles as hegemon and regional protector, and as global challenger and regional hegemonic aspirant, they go through a series of crises, some of which are militarized (and concern maritime disputes between China and its smaller neighbors). Each crisis leaves traces in the thinking of either side, cements the idea that the counterpart is the destined adversary, and leads to additional efforts to improve one's own military posture in case that things come to a head.

After a long lull in Chinese-Taiwanese tensions, China's leadership, confronted with domestic turmoil and in need of visible success, enhances pressures on the Taiwanese to come to agree to reintegration into the PRC rather than dragging its feet on reunification forever. Inevitably, this strengthens the hand of Taiwanese nationalists. Supported by a recession, the nationalists come to power on the ticket of independence and move energetically to realize this goal. When talks with the US remain unsatisfactory, they take the plunge and declare independence without US backing.

China's leadership is irate and mobilizes for war in the expectation that US policy – defending Taiwan against an unprovoked Chinese attack, but standing aloof when Taipei claims sovereignty unilaterally – continues. The Republican president in Washington is under pressure from his party's right wing commanding both Senate and House, and from exponents of the security establishment and the military leadership who think the US position will be fatally damaged in the region and globally if it refuses to protect Taiwan against a Chinese assault.

The US president concedes. He sends three aircraft carrier groups towards East Asia, puts forces in the region on high alert, and heightens the alert status of all US forces worldwide. Countries in the region, sensing the high tension, go to higher alert status as well. The US allies Australia, Japan, and South Korea do this at once, North Korea follows, then ASEAN countries with a direct conflict with China, then Russia (which wants to keep military flexibility in a high-flux situation), then India (just in case), and Pakistan as a corollary. The fuse is ready to ignite the powder. An explosion may be triggered by preemptive attack according to the strategies of the two main protagonists or by the maverick action of some "spoiler."

Scenario II: The South China Sea problem

The second scenario emerges from increasing assertiveness of China in the South China Sea, expressed through a growing naval presence and the demonstrative occupation and military buildup on some of the disputed islands. The Philippines and Vietnam become increasingly restive; the number and intensity of naval skirmishes increase until China finally moves towards deciding the issue through a major operation against the navies of its smaller neighbors. Nearly all of ASEAN (pro-Chinese Cambodia excluded) is highly concerned. Under Malaysian and Indonesian influence, ASEAN does not ask for US support (a move seen as risky and contrary to ASEAN philosophy), but turns rather to India, whose naval position on the Andamans seems to give advantages over China, and may suffice to bring China to the negotiation table. China, however, pushes its case and does not only take on the Indian navy, but also moves troops into Southern Tibet, threatening the Indian position in Arunachal Pradesh, while Pakistan tries to seize the opportunity of a vastly diverted India to make another attempt against Kashmir. The Indian navy is – unexpectedly – badly mauled near the Malacca Strait, and the Indians call for US assistance to rescue them.

Again, the US is in a difficult position. Giving in delivers the South China Sea and the whole of ASEAN to its global rival and leaves India, an essential continental balancer and fellow democracy, much weakened. The US navy and air force attempting to contain Chinese expansion in the South China

Sea, however, may trigger Chinese countermeasures more to the North, towards Japan, South Korea, and/or Taiwan, with a high potential for horizontal escalation from Kashmir to the Japanese islands.

Discussion

The two scenarios were discussed skeleton-wise. They can be made worse by maverick actions by potential spoilers: It is not unreasonable to imagine Pakistan attacking Kashmir or North Korea asserting its own importance by shelling a South Korean island or sinking a South Korean ship; these are acts that have been committed before. In addition, there are manifold contingencies emerging from naval and air forces being on alert and operating in close proximity to each other. The Cuban missile crisis showed that these factors can have enormous repercussions on the course of events without political authorities being aware of the dangers before it is too late. Lastly, there is the instability problem resulting from the preemptive strategies by the two protagonists, and each side's inevitable fear of falling victim to preemption if it waits too long.

The worrisome message of this analysis is not fully borne out by pointing to the inherent instability of the more conflicting and competitive dyads; even the best available analysis of inherent instabilities in the US-China relationship is limited to dyadic analysis.[32] A crisis with a potential for degenerating into actual fighting in any of the many disputes across the regional complex may have repercussions across the whole conflict system. Such a crisis, therefore, might force actors with no particular stakes in a specific conflict to consider reacting because of the consequences that an undesirable outcome would have for one's own core national interests.

Military tensions between China and the United States could concern the vital interests of actors across the interconnected theaters. As a consequence, all national forces will go to higher alert in order to be prepared. Higher alert rates for conventional forces will be followed or accompanied by nuclear powers enhancing the readiness of their nuclear forces. In a multipolar deterrence system, the six nuclear powers racing towards high alert rates could combine to weaken whatever stability might be afforded by nuclear

---

[32] Avery Goldstein, "First Things First. The Pressing Danger of Crisis Instability in U.S.-China Relations," *International Security* 37/4 (2013).

deterrence, turning the nuclear postures of the participants from instruments of self-reassurance to dangerous liabilities.[33]

Management tools: Proposing a modern day concert of powers

Considering the conflict constellation and the escalation scenarios, what would be needed in order to minimize the risk of a great power war is a security institution in which the various security problems of and among the great powers could be discussed and resolved.

We are thus looking for an instrument offering something to rising powers, while at the same time staying attractive for the declining dominant power and the great powers in general. While searching for such an arrangement, one may strike gold in the pages of history concerning the idea of a concert of powers. In a concert system, great powers collaborate continuously and in an institutionalized but not necessarily formal way in order to keep peace among themselves and to manage change and stability within an international order.[34] While the Concert of Europe did not prevent World War I, this is no reason to ignore its achievements in the 19th and early 20th centuries.[35] The European Concert did a remarkable job in its 100 years of existence. Even though it did not prevent all wars, it rendered the 19th century the least bellicose century in the "Great-Power System" of the modern era. This relative peacefulness suggests that we may find some guiding principles there for a working security system today.

The European Concert was or is – of course – not the only attempt to manage and stabilize the international order. In the interwar period the League of Nations and after the World War II the United Nations offered alternative

---

[33] Sumit Ganguly and William R. Thompson, *Asian rivalries: Conflict, escalation, and limitations on two-level games* (Stanford, CA: Stanford University Press 2011).

[34] In calling for a concert of powers, we depart from PTT: we see the key to great power peace not exclusively in the relations between the dominant power and the rising challenger. Usually systems are stratified, with a small group of relevant states in the upper echelon. Hence, in addition to hegemon and challenger, there are minor but still significant powers that PTT neglects. Putting them in the picture reveals the need for a multilateral management template.

[35] Schulz, *Normen*; Paul W. Schroeder, *The Transformation of European Politics 1763-1848* (Oxford: Clarendon Press 1994).

approaches. The League, however, was unsuccessful in keeping the international order stable and prevented neither individual acts of aggression against other member states by Germany, Italy, and Japan in the 1930s and the Soviet attack against Finland in 1939, nor World War II. Today there is no shortage of international institutions, but institutional tools to deal with the challenge of a seminal power change plus manifold great power conflicts appear insufficient. Of course, there are institutions meant to manage international security. Global security problems are supposed to be discussed and solved in the United Nations Security Council (UNSC). However, while the UN system has been more successful than its predecessor, the UNSC's membership still represents the power structure of 1945 and is thus – without meaningful reform – part of the problem. Furthermore, the formal and politicized setting contributes to the tendency of the P5 to cast the veto when solutions go beyond their narrowly defined interests instead of continuing deliberation in order to seek compromises acceptable for all.

Other existing institutions fare no better: The G-8, which has extended its agenda from mere economics to some security issues, is even more constrained in terms of membership. Russia was kicked out because of Moscow's moves against Ukraine concerning Crimea. Furthermore, China, the most important rising power, is not a member; the same holds true for India. The G20 reflects a better balance than either the UNSC or the G-8, but it is confined to an economic agenda. Contact groups had some limited successes e.g. in dealing with the nuclear crises concerning Iran and North Korea. They include all powers concerned, but they are rather ad-hoc and problem-specific. It is unlikely that a contact group (assembling actors that feel responsible for its specific purpose) is able to deal with the interwoven complexities of modern great power conflicts.

What is lacking is a forum dedicated to international security that involves all contemporary great powers. History does not offer many successful structures of this kind. A framework that has been reasonably successful in stabilizing and pacifying a multipolar environment was the European Concert in the 19th century.[36]

---

[36] Moreover, in comparison to other types of peaceful systems that were either based on a hegemonic (East Asian system from ca 1200 to ca 1700) or bipolar structure (post-WW II world), the Concert was run as an institutionalized management system among equals and therefore seems much more similar to the present time.

The post-Vienna system, of which the concert was an integral part, was devised by the victorious powers of the Napoleonic wars, with the aim of preventing the recurrence of deadly great power clashes.[37] The new order was built on new norms, cultural practices, agreements, and institutional devices. These included the multilateral treaty order agreed upon at the Congress of Vienna, frequent monarchical encounters, meetings of foreign ministers and ambassadors, and the Vienna diplomatic protocol, which reduced conflicts about questions of rank and prestige. Members guaranteed their mutual existence and territorial integrity and recognized each other's vital interests. They agreed upon equal treatment of member states with different capabilities. All of them undertook not to change the status quo by force and not to intervene in other member states´ internal affairs, except by diplomatic means. Furthermore, they were united by the common objective of containing revisionist ambitions. Most importantly, however, was the practice of collective consultation (as an instrument for crisis management) and common action.

This Concert of Europe, incredibly successful from 1815 to the Crimean War of 1854, and reasonably effective afterwards – containing the wars of Italian and German unification and keeping peace among the European great powers until the eve of the Great War – was still not completely dysfunctional in the second decade of the 20th century.[38] The management of the Balkan troubles in 1908, 1912, and 1913 displayed the Concert's toolbox for the last time, preserving peace beyond what would have been possible in a simple great power balancing game. Unfortunately, these tools were left unused in 1914. Paul Schroeder's argument that the Great War resulted less from what governments did but what they did not – using the instruments at hand for dispute management – gains considerable traction.[39] The Concert suffered from the diminishing willingness of Great Britain to play its role as the prudent balancer that kept an eye on the preservation of the status of all the great power partners. Britain grew increasingly disinterested in the status of the Danube Monarchy, while France and Russia were working on its

---

[37] Schulz, *Normen*.

[38] Some scholars identify the Crimean War as the endpoint of the concert (Andreas Hillgruber, *Bismarcks Außenpolitik*, Rombach-Hochschul-Paperback 46, 1. Aufl (Freiburg: Rombach 1972)). Others maintain that it prevented this war from becoming a world war and stayed active for the rest of the century and even up to World War I (Schulz, *Normen*).

[39] Paul W. Schroeder, *System, Stability, and Statecraft* (Houndmills-Basingstoke: Palgrave Macmillan 2004), Chapter 7.

dismantlement and Germany was supporting it à l'outrance as its only remaining ally. The instruments of Concert diplomacy, developed and preserved by three generation of leaders and diplomats, laid idle when they were needed most.

Naturally, studies of the concert have been done mainly by historians but IR has also taken notice of the concert approach.[40] In doing so, IR theories appraise the European Concert quite differently. Realists usually explain the cooperation between the great powers in Europe and the absence of war during much of the concert period as successful application of balance-of-power politics.[41] On the other hand, many scholars see the Concert of Europe as the major paradigmatic case of a strong and effective international institution in the area of security governance.[42] According to the standard description provided by both historians and international relations specialists, the norms and rules of the Concert accounted for an unusually high degree of security cooperation among all the European great powers.[43] Paul W. Schroeder, a leading diplomatic historian of the Concert period, argues against the realist position. He points out that "the allies chose moral, legal, and political means rather than balance of power measures to maintain a balance in this vital respect."[44]

---

[40] See: Schulz, Normen, 20-29, for a concise overview over the current state of research.

[41] Branislav L. Slantchev, "Territory and Commitment: The Concert of Europe as Self—Enforcing Equilibrium," Security Studies 14/4 (2005), Korina Kagan, "The Myth of the European Concert: The Realist-Institutionalist Debate and Great Power Behavior in the Eastern Question, 1821–41," Security Studies 7/2 (1997).

[42] Institutionalist analyses of the Concert belong to both the liberal and the constructivist school.

[43] Robert Jervis, "From Balance to Concert: A study of International Security Cooperation," World Politics 38/1 (1985), Robert Jervis, "A Political Science Perspective on the Balance of Power and the Concert," The American Historical Review 97/3 (1992), Charles A. Kupchan and Clifford A. Kupchan, "Concerts, Collective Security, and the Future of Europe," International Security 16/1 (1991), Charles Kupchan, How Enemies Become Friends - The Sources of Stable Peace (Princeton, NJ: Princeton Univ. Press 2010), Jennifer Mitzen, Power in concert: The nineteenth-century origins of global governance (Chicago, London: University of Chicago Press 2013).

[44] Paul W. Schroeder, "Did the Vienna Settlement Rest on a Balance of Power?" The American Historical Review 97/3 (1992), 698. Also see: Paul W. Schroeder, Austria, Great Britain, and the Crimean War: The destruction of the European concert (Ithaca, NY: Cornell University Press 1972), Paul W. Schroeder, "The 19th Century International System: Changes in the Structure," World Politics 39/1 (1986), Schroeder, Transformation.

In a comprehensive way, the state of the art on the European Concert is represented by Matthias Schulz's study, which covers the whole period of 1815 through 1860, with some accounts reaching to the eve of World War I.[45] Schulz ends the confusion between the Concert and the Holy Alliance, which has led scores of scholars to ascribe a reactionary bias to the former, by explaining not only the difference in institution and membership, but also proving in great detail how the Concert managed change – such as the vindication of nationalist movements through the creation of a new nation-state – for Belgium, Greece, and Romania, and smoothened the unlikely transfer of the province of Neufchatel from Prussian into Swiss possession.

On the basis of what scholarly work tells us about the European Concert, why it worked and why it decayed in the end, we conclude that it is a template worthy of thorough scrutiny when it comes to the task of arranging great power relations in today's world.

Several features of the European Concert, however, were already problematic during its time and would be unacceptable, dysfunctional, and counterproductive in the modern world (for example, its notorious exclusivity[46] and lack of accountability and the simultaneous restraint in Europe and violent expansion in the rest of the world, bolstered by the racist and inhuman categorization of the world into "civilized" and "uncivilized" people). This advises us to very carefully examine the risks of international hierarchy and exclusivity and to devise methods of overcoming these risks.[47] Regarding substance, it is also hard to imagine in today's world regulating great power relations without agreed regimes of arms control that were not a part of the European Concert. Thus, it is clear that despite its achievements, the European Concert cannot be simply transferred or copied to today. We prefer to speak about a template or inspiration rather than about a blueprint. Yet insights into the normative and procedural basis for the Concert's achievements offer useful hints on how to structure great power cooperation in our time.

---

[45] Schulz, Normen.
[46] This point is also raised in Kupchan and Kupchan's otherwise quite friendly analysis of the Concert as a collective security: "One final disadvantage of a concert is its exclusivity," Kupchan and Kupchan, "Concerts," 144.
[47] See: Bertrand Badie, La Diplomatie de Connivence - Les Dérives Oligarchiques du Système International (Paris: Découverte 2011).

As an institution tailor-made for the security challenges of the 21st century, a modernized concert should have the following objectives: First, to prevent or de-escalate conflicts between the great powers and between great powers and smaller states that may draw other great powers in. But it would also aim to (i) maintain a political equilibrium characterized by restraint and acceptance of other powers' interests and a mutual recognition that security is interdependent; (ii) facilitate common activities in areas related to security; and (iii) create conditions for common activities in regard of other governance problems.[48]

We do not develop the idea of how such a modern day concert might look in detail in this article.[49] But let us say that "concertation," in our understanding, means a commitment among the leading powers to consult regularly in an attempt to harmonize differing positions in order to develop common approaches; first, to avoid tensions among themselves that threaten to escalate towards military confrontation and, second, to reach understanding among themselves in multilateral institutions on issues of global interest. Apart from this skeleton definition that covers the European Concert as well as a modernized version, a modern concert of powers cannot just copy the historical one; instead, it should build on the European Concert's successful norms and practices while adding new principles to make it fit for the 21st century. Most important would be norms about accepting diversity between members, renouncing ambitions of military superiority, and granting respect, voice, and responsibility to non-members.[50]

In order to work successfully, it would have to grant both rising and existing great powers a voice in any emerging world order, in a fashion recognized as legitimate by lesser powers.[51] It would also have to allow great powers with

---

[48] Ibid., 22.
[49] Interested readers might take a look at the policy paper authored collectively by an international study group to which the authors of this text contributed. The 21st Century Concert Study Group, A Twenty-First Century Concert of Powers: Promoting Great Power Multilateralism for the Post-Transatlantic Era (Frankfurt am Main: Peace Research Institute Frankfurt 2014).
[50] We deal with these norms in more detail elsewhere: Müller and Rauch, Machtübergangsmanagement, Harald Müller, Daniel Müller, Konstanze Jüngling and Carsten Rauch, Ein Mächtekonzert für das 21. Jahrhundert – Blaupause für eine von Großmächten getragene multilaterale Sicherheitsinstitution, HSFK-Report 1/2014 (Frankfurt am Main: Hessische Stiftung Friedens- und Konfliktforschung 2014), also see: The 21st Century Concert Study Group, Twenty, 52–60.
[51] The question of membership will be a political and not an academic one, but it is safe to assume that it would be impossible to establish a concert without the United States,

different ideologies, histories, and cultural heritages to grow accustomed to each other in a non-confrontational setting. It has to provide a forum in which informal consultation can take place, away from the constraints and protocols of existing multilateral fora such as the UNSC and less exclusive than existing informal fora such as the G7 or G8, and it would have to foster shared understanding and a common sense of responsibility among great powers.

To sum up: A concert for the 21st century should be based on the norms of its 19th century predecessor while adding some crucial new norms. It should be a complement instead of an alternative to existing international institutions. It should be more informal than the UNSC and more inclusive and balanced than both the UNSC and the G8. Established in such a fashion, a modernized great power concert could build on the achievements of the European Concert while eschewing its shortcomings.

Conclusion: Make Concert, Not War

Whether in Syria, the East or South China Sea, or the Ukraine: the world today is ripe with security challenges involving or at least concerning several great powers. At the same time, the ramifications of a war between modern (mostly nuclear-armed) great powers go beyond anything that humankind has experienced before and could end in the collapse of civilization. The "end of history"[52] has to be cancelled, but the "return of history"[53] does not inevitably mean war. Mankind is not doomed to repeat 1914. Not even in 1914 was war the only possible outcome, as Lebow argues in a series of counterfactuals.[54] If the past was contingent, the future will be even more so. Preserving peace, however, will not be a no-brainer. Neither nuclear deterrence, nor democracy, nor the obsolescence of major war can guarantee peace and stability. Just as in the Cold War, during which the world more than once just barely scraped past the outbreak of a hot war, it will

---

Russia, China, and India. Besides this core group, members should be added for reasons of their (potential) weight in world politics as well as for reasons of (regional) balance.

[52] Francis Fukuyama, *The End of History and the Last Man* (London: Hamilton 1992).
[53] Robert Kagan, *The Return of History and the End of Dreams* (London: Atlantic Books 2008).
[54] Richard N. Lebow, *Archduke Franz Ferdinand lives!: A world without World War I* (Basingstoke: Palgrave Macmillan 2014).

require hard work and the volition of the central actors, most importantly the great powers.

The establishment of a 21st century Concert of Powers, which aims to bring together the declining hegemon, rising powers, and the group of great powers in general in an informal setting, could support this effort.

While one could argue the recent re-emergence of previously overcome hostile relations between the West and Russia concerning the Ukraine crisis makes a concert of powers less likely, we want to stress that precisely developments like this underline the importance of great power "concertation." Russian ambitions to dominate the "near abroad" and Western enthusiasm for the Euromaidan movement aside, it appears obvious that the interpretation of the aftermath of the EU-brokered agreement between the Yanukovych government and the opposition of February 20th 2014 demonstrates a serious lack of trust between Washington, Brussels, and Moscow. Great power consultation in a concert setting is meant to defuse such distrust. At the very least, increased consultation is more conductive to conflict resolution than the opposite, decreased consultation. Unfortunately, it is the latter that seems to be the knee-jerk Western response to Russia's actions on Crimea and Ukraine. While the conflict between Russia and the West is the more immediate case, the rise of China is probably the more crucial one. Soothing the relations between the declining hegemon and the rising challenger, while at the same time keeping all major powers in contact and communication, would be the concert's most vital task.

If the participants decide to abandon concert diplomacy (as the European great powers had chosen to do by 1914), a concert cannot ascertain peace and the functionality of the concert will break down. But if the great powers stick together, a concert can maximize *the chances* for peace.

Ernst Barlach, "Magdeburger Ehrenmal" ("Magdeburg Memorial")

German soldiers on a battlefield, World War I

The New Major Powers of Asia: Will Their Strategic Choices and Preferences Overshadow the West? Drawing Lessons from 1914

Namrata Goswami

Abstract:

The gradual but definitive influence of China and India on the global stage is increasing, along with their role in economic and financial institutions. The establishment of the BRICS Development Bank in 2014 is a case in point. This chapter discusses the internal strategic logic of both China and India and explains how their strategic choices will shape their preferences. China is motivated by three significant strategic priorities, namely: ensuring its strategic presence in East Asia, establishing itself as a power of reckoning in Asia, and showcasing its power and reach outside the geopolitics of Asia. India, on the other hand, is focused on improving bilateral relationship with the US and dealing with the rise of China. This chapter posits that, while there will be competing claims for legitimacy and relevance within Asia between the ideational influences of the pluralistic underpinnings of Indian democracy and the authoritarian single mindedness of China, there will be no single Asian alliance against the West, but rather alliances and partnerships based on mutual interests and threat perceptions.

China's Strategic Choices and its Preferences

China has risen. With an economy that is instrumental for much of the world's economic growth and a military that can broadcast its power across the world, debates about whether China will break up like the Soviet Union or whether it will start a downward slide are irrelevant in the present context. Rather, it is critical to understand China's strategic choices and what kind of preferences these choices are giving shape to. Amongst the strategic choices that China has owned up to in the last few years, three are of priority.

1. Maintain strategic presence in East Asia.
2. Establish itself as a power of reckoning in Asia.
3. Showcase its power and reach outside the geopolitics of Asia.

Strategic Presence in East Asia

China's first choice as a major power is to showcase its power and presence in East Asia. This broadcasting of power has historical overtones, as China was a major ideational influence on countries like Japan and South Korea, with Confucianism and Buddhism spreading from China to the furthest corners of Northeast Asia. The spread of Chinese script had a major role in streamlining Japanese and Korean scripts. While assertion of Japanese identity in the late 19th and early 20th centuries took on destructive dimensions with the invasion of Manchuria and China, this retelling of history and China's decision, not just aspiration, to be the primary power in East Asia is the core of its foreign policy choices. In this strategic choice, the presence of the US, a wartime ally, has complicated things. It was Franklin D. Roosevelt who ensured that China was included on the high table after the end of the Second World War, as well as enabling it to play a major role in the formation of the United Nations.[1] While Taiwan or the Republic of China represented China in the UN after the Communist takeover of China in 1949 under Mao Tse Tung, this was undone after Nixon's famous visit to China in 1972. China has not forgotten these overtures by the US to include it as part of the international system. However, while gratitude is an important dimension of human behavior, interests that propel strategic choices are a critical dimension of state behavior as well. Hence, states will always want to shape their immediate geopolitical environment to their liking. China's anxiety is that the presence of the US as a net provider of international security in East Asia is a threat to China's calculus of maturity and its historical wisdom. China sees and interprets the US presence not as a net provider of security, but as a fence to limit China's rise and influence its strategic choices. For instance, China views the US-Japan or the US-South Korean relationships not as relationships that are mutually self-explanatory, but as only sustaining their

---

[1] "China's Emergence as a Great Power Began with FDR", Roosevelt Institute, <http://www.rooseveltinstitute.org/new-roosevelt/china-s-emergence-great-power-began-fdr>.

robustness and vitality by functioning in a strategic space that views China as the adversary.

As a result, one of China's subset of strategic choices is to reset the calculation of risks in East Asia by casting doubts on the US's capability to protect East Asian allies for lesser contingencies[2] by declaring an Air Defense Identification Zone (ADIZ), thus orchestrating a major role in the Association of Southeast Asian Nations (ASEAN), the East Asia Summit (EAS), and the Shanghai Cooperation Organization (SCO). These strategic postures, where military power broadcasting is a major component, are a serious challenge to the East Asian regional order, limiting the US to symbolically reassuring its allies by, for example, flying B-52 bombers over the Chinese ADIZ. With a faltering economy and military sequestration, the US is forced to ensure that its military presence in East Asia does not recede from its present strength, contrary to the expectations that the "Asian pivot"[3] gave rise to: that the US will increase its military strength in Asia.

This strategic choice by China has cast doubts on whether the East Asian order will be peaceful; that conflict is inevitable since a major local power is seemingly hostile to the presence of the US. However, Chinese scholars reflect that conflict may not be inevitable because China, while wanting to sensitize the US to its own strategic choice of increased presence in East Asia, is not gunning to start a war. This assumption is inferred from the visit by President Xi Jingping to the US in February 2012, when both he and President Obama agreed to prioritize mutual common referral points based on trust-building and familiarize American politicians with Xi's political, economic, ideological, and diplomatic preferences. There was a momentum to consolidate Sino-US trade relations and to establish mechanisms that can reduce strategic misunderstandings.[4]

---

[2] Rajan Menon, "China Ascendant: Is Conflict Inevitable?" The National Interest, December 17, 2013, <http://nationalinterest.org/commentary/china-ascendant-conflict-inevitable-9576?page=5>.

[3] Kurt Campbell and Brian Andrews, "Explaining the US 'Pivot' to Asia", Chatham House, August 2013, <http://www.chathamhouse.org/sites/default/files/public/Research/Americas/0813pp_pivottoasia.pdf>.

[4] Yuhan Zhang and Lin Shi, "Conflict between China and the US is not Inevitable", East Asia Forum, April 13, 2013, <http://www.eastasiaforum.org/2013/04/13/conflict-between-china-and-the-us-is-not-inevitable/>.

If one envisions a military conflict in East Asia, the greatest fear is that it will not remain limited but will spiral out of control in a zone containing nuclear weapons. This is dangerous given the military strength of China and the US, as well as of lesser powers like Japan, South Korea, Vietnam, etc. One cannot be too sure that in a fight between the US and China, Vietnam will automatically take the US's side. The plausible intervening variable if a China-US conflict ensues is that Japan may be forced to change its Article 9, which limits its defense capabilities and structures. However, this may not be a major factor, as it takes time to prepare an offense-based military. There are rumblings that the East Asian regional order is becoming conflict-prone because of Japan's jealousy with China's economic rise, a status that Japan wanted to clinch for itself but lost after its economic bubble in the 1990s.

In its calculation of risks and strategic choice for larger visible presence in East Asia, China's leadership has to showcase maturity and carve a path that leads towards global prestige and not a backslide.[5] Offensive realists like John Mearsheimer argue that the US and China will go to war because the US faces real existential challenge to its own prestige and presence in Asia due to China's rise/resurgence. On the other hand, a cold war between the US and China will be similar to the US-Soviet Cold War, though the strategic competition will be even more intense and the center of geopolitical gravity will be East Asia rather than Europe during the Cold War. In all likelihood, this conflict will turn nuclear. The four flashpoints in this inevitable conflict based on a Cold War pattern will be the Korean Peninsula, Taiwan Straits, and the South and East China Seas. Mearsheimer believes that if a conflict breaks out between Japan and China, the US can either act as a referee or enter the conflict on the side of Japan. Mearsheimer perhaps does not realize that the Chinese conflict calculus is not really targeted at Japan, but at the US. So, to suggest that the US can act as a referee is shortsighted at best. Therefore, Mearsheimer's second option, that the US will enter the war on behalf of Japan, holds more water, as a failure to do so would weaken US credibility and limit its influence in the calculation of its Asian allies. Mearsheimer himself goes on to argue that the US will choose the second option as insurance against either Japan or South Korea building their nuclear arsenals. But this logic is not self-explanatory as to how a weakening US, with limited capability to assert its presence in East Asia, will motivate its

---

[5] Michael Sutton, "War with China is not Inevitable, So Tread Carefully", Japan Times, April 03, 2013, <http://www.japantimes.co.jp/opinion/2013/04/03/commentary/japan-commentary/war-with-china-is-not-inevitable-so-tread-carefully/#.U4nhAHKSyxo>.

allies to shore up their own defense potential, including a step towards nuclear weaponization. Mearsheimer hopes that all these scenarios will not pan out as the Chinese economy may lose its sheen and power by 2050; he expresses his frustration at the US's and its allied states' willingness to ensure the Chinese economic growth and their playing a major supportive role in that endeavor as a result. For him, a Chinese economy growing at the GDP growth rates of Singapore or Taiwan is a major threat to the US.[6]

The Chinese Academy of Social Sciences believes that Chinese-Japanese relations are not stable, especially with the hawkish Japanese Prime Minister, Shinzo Abe, coming to power. Notably, the Academy posits that China's rapid development is causing tensions in its neighborhood, especially pertaining to the readjustment in power balance that China is seeking to orchestrate. As for Japan's stand on the issue, the Academy believes that with the ascendance of right wing groups in Japan under Abe, Japan would view this moment as offering the best opportunity to nationalize the disputed Senkaku/Diaoyu Islands, by taking advantage of the US "pivot" to Asia policy.[7] To counter this, China's strategic choice is to "up the ante" in these island chains to ensure that Japan does not run away with the impression that it has hold on them.

One of the more tragic inferences from this Chinese assertion in East Asia is that it will result in a 1914-like scenario. While it is likely that this comparison will be made, given our penchant for remembering or celebrating bicentenaries and centenaries, sometimes with ill-intended consequences, it is unlikely that tensions about power and prestige will result in a World War III between China on one hand and the US along with its allies on the other. Besides the sobering influence of nuclear weapons, it is important to remember that the amount of diplomatic mechanisms and economic interdependence that exist between China and the US is perhaps unprecedented in history. Under the aegis of the Strategic and Economic Dialogue, around 1000 officials from most departments and ministries between the two countries meet every year. Issues where collaboration has emerged include disaster relief, humanitarian aid, and joint training of Afghan

---

[6] Zachary Keck, "US-China rivalry more dangerous than Cold War?" The Diplomat, January 28, 2014, <http://thediplomat.com/2014/01/us-china-rivalry-more-dangerous-than-cold-war/>.

[7] Nozomo Hayashi, "Chinese think tank: Conflict Inevitable between Japan, China over Senkaku," The Asahi Shimbun, December 31, 2012, <http://ajw.asahi.com/article/asia/china/AJ201212310012>.

diplomats. This is in stark contrast to the period preceding 1914, when there were hardly any worthwhile meetings between Britain and Germany. Moreover, multilateral frameworks in Asia such as ASEAN and the Asia-Pacific Economic Cooperation (APEC) have brought about meetings between heads of states even on contentious issues, for instance that of a Code of Conduct (CoC) in the South China Sea.[8] These multilateral forums will work against any war that will endanger the peace in Asia that fosters prosperity.[9]

China as a Power to Reckon With in Asia

China, as we know, has been a historical great power, establishing a tributary system, spreading its influence and its culture, and aspiring to be the middle kingdom with a mandate from heaven. While the period from the late 19th to the early 20th century is viewed in China as resulting in 100 years of humiliation with Western and Japanese intervention in the internal affairs of China, the late 20th and early 21st centuries has reinstated China as a major power in international politics. It also has global ambitions, as evidenced by its quest for resources in Africa and Latin America, its prowess in South Asia and Myanmar, its economic energy in Southeast Asia and Europe, and its reach into the US economy. Recently, China announced the establishment of a US $50 billion Asian Infrastructure Investment Bank (AIIB) to boost regional connectivity and economic cooperation, in contrast to the World Bank and the Asian Development Bank (ADB) whose thrust is on poverty reduction. This initiative was announced by President Xi Jinping and Premier Li Keqiang in October 2013.[10] China is a member of the G-20, using it as an important platform to discuss issues and striking common ground with the US whenever possible and discussing critical issues like US-China economic

---

[8] "It's Not 1914 all over again: Asia is preparing to avoid war," The Conversation, March 10, 2014, <http://theconversation.com/its-not-1914-all-over-again-asia-is-preparing-to-avoid-war-22875>.

[9] Namrata Goswami, "Analysts Reckless in Claiming Similarities to WWI Scenario," Global Times, February 06, 2014, <http://www.globaltimes.cn/content/840948.shtml> (Accessed on March 21, 2014).

[10] "China Starts Work on US $ 50 billion Asia Infrastructure Bank," Reuters, March 07, 2014,
<http://www.reuters.com/article/2014/03/07/china-bank-idUSL3N0M42NQ20140307>.

reforms and their bilateral debt situation.[11] China is one of the main architects, along with India, Russia, and South Africa, of the recently established BRICS Development Bank with headquarters in Shanghai.[12]

It can be clearly inferred that China is asserting its military power in Asia. This can be seen from the way the scenario is unfolding, which is not just about military power-balancing but also about identity, prestige, and pride. This assertion was explicitly seen in China's announcement of the ADIZ and in a statement by one of its military commanders that China will take military action against any foreign aircraft that violates the ADIZ. This naturally brought on a response from the US, which stated that the Chinese ADIZ is a provocation of Japan and its allies in the region. As mentioned earlier, to further vindicate its stand, the US flew two B-52 bombers across the disputed islands and right through the Chinese ADIZ. US allies like Japan and South Korea followed suit by sending their surveillance aircraft into the area. Significantly, China sent its warplanes to patrol the ADIZ.[13] It is indeed fascinating to unravel the deeper psychological reasons behind the escalation of tensions in the East China Seas. Interwoven into claims and counterclaims are personal egos and personal reasons. Japanese Prime Minister Shinzo Abe's grandfather had administered Japanese Manchuria in the 1930s, right about the time President Xi's father was taking part in the Chinese Communist Party (CCP)'s fight against the Japanese forces. That background explains why the territorial assertion is about China projecting itself as a power to reckon with in Asia, especially to neighboring Japan. It was clear after Xi came to power that China's claim over disputed territories will be shored up.[14]

The deeper question lurking behind this is whether China's emergence as a dominant player in Asia and the world would result in a new world war[15]: whether we would like to highlight the story of the *Titanic,* which sank, or the

---

[11] "China, US Argue Economic Reform at G20 Meeting," Peoples' Daily, February 26, 2014, <http://english.people.com.cn/98649/8546831.html>.

[12] Unmesh Rajendran, "BRICS Bank: The New Kid on the Block," The Diplomat, July 28, 2014, <http://thediplomat.com/2014/07/brics-bank-the-new-kid-on-the-block/>.

[13] "China Sends Warplanes to Newly Declared Air Zone," BBC News, November 28, 2013, <http://www.bbc.com/news/world-asia-china-25144465>.

[14] Allan Topol, "War with China," Huffington Post, December 10, 2013, <http://www.huffingtonpost.com/allan-topol/war-with-china_1_b_4412585.html>.

[15] James G. Wiles, "Will 2014 See a Repeat of 1914?" American Thinker, December 29, 2013,
<http://www.americanthinker.com/2013/12/will_2014_see_a_repeat_of_1914.html>.

Olympic, a ship made by the same company that safely made its way across the oceans; whether we would like to highlight the conflicting situations or the cooperative ones, is a matter of interpretation. [16]

It is perhaps wise to avoid the reductionist inferences from 1914, especially when they may not explain the events of today, or turn events of today into a self-fulfilling prophecy. History is a great instructor, but history may not necessarily repeat itself.[17] While China is indeed interested in demonstrating its growing power potential, I argue that this will not result in a conflict similar to what we had in 1914 for the sole reason that this demonstration of power is perhaps acceptable to the US, given its own decline in economic strength and the war fatigue felt by the American population. Nevertheless, there have been suggestions that the tensions over the Senkaku/Diaoyu Islands in East China Sea will result in a similar situation to the Sarajevo incident that provoked a World War I. Very unlikely, unless, of course, there arises a situation akin to the killing of the Archduke Franz Ferdinand of Austria that led to World War I, something dramatic and on an equal scale, in Asia. Given the current state of high personal security for leaders like Xi and Abe, this scenario seems highly improbable.

Drawing parallels between two scenarios that are actually dissimilar has negative consequences and suffers from the methodical error of "overdetermination." Moreover, even if one wants to compare both periods, it is important to realize that World War I did not occur accidentally. Germany had already been planning on a war due to the rising Russian threat in the East, French and British threats in the West, and instability and unrest at home. Consequently, the economic interdependence that is so trumpeted about before World War I did not have the effect it is credited with enjoying: that of interdependence trumping warlike tendencies. China's motivation and rationale today are different than Germany's then. China is motivated to project its power in the East Asian neighborhood and beyond, through a combination of economics, politics, and military prowess. Given the fact that China has benefited from both regional and international economic arrangements and political institutions, a peaceful regional and international

---

[16] Adam Gopnik, "Two Ships," The New Yorker, January 06, 2014, <http://www.newyorker.com/talk/comment/2014/01/06/140106taco_talk_gopnik>.

[17] Christopher Clark, "Echoes of 1914: Are Today's Conflicts a case of History Repeating Itself?" The Guardian, January 16, 2014,
<http://www.theguardian.com/world/2014/jan/15/1914-conflicts-history-repeating-first-world-war>.

order is much more to its benefit internally or otherwise. Consequently, it is rather unlikely that China will engage in the kind of conflict that Germany did in 1914. It is equally true that World War I broke out because of the diplomatic failures preceding it, unlike in the case of China, which was heavily invested in diplomatic maneuvers and political interconnectedness. One of the fault lines in this aspect could be the absence of a major naval agreement between China and the US to avoid confrontation at sea, but efforts are underway through mechanisms like ASEAN and EAS to deal with concepts like the freedom of the Sea Lanes of Communication (SLOCs) and avoid conflict in the vital economic lifelines of Asia. It is unlikely that China will engage in naval conflict, especially in areas like the Malacca Strait, its lifeline for the flow of food, energy and all other exported goods.[18]

Showcase China's Power and Reach outside Asia

Fascinatingly, China's increasing aim now is to showcase its power outside of Asian geopolitics. In order to operationalize this in practice, China has started making its presence felt in global institutions such as the World Trade Organization, the International Monetary Fund, the SCO, the African Union, BRICS, and the G20. China has invested heavily in Africa, significantly not just limited to mining, infrastructure, and energy but also in health, education, and cultural projects. China's diplomacy in Africa is largely motivated by a desire to promote good relations and trading in raw materials.[19] While there are lingering questions about China's intentions in Africa, whether they are based on investment or exploitation, the scale and depth of Chinese investment is pretty large.[20] China is playing a major role in the G20 as well, utilizing it as a platform to showcase power and influence, debating issues

---

[18] Paul Dibb, "Why 2014 in Asia Will Not be a Repeat of 1914 in Europe," ISN ETH Zurich, April 03, 2014, <http://isnblog.ethz.ch/conflict/why-2014-in-asia-will-not-be-a-repeat-of-1914-in-europe>.

[19] Claire Provost and Rich Harris, "China Commits Billions in Aid to Africa as Part of Charm Offensive-Interactive," The Guardian, April 29, 2013, <http://www.theguardian.com/global-development/interactive/2013/apr/29/china-commits-billions-aid-africa-interactive>.

[20] "China in Africa: Investment or Exploitation?" Al Jazeera, May 04, 2014, <http://www.aljazeera.com/programmes/insidestory/2014/05/china-africa-investment-exploitation-201454154158396626.html>.

concerning the world economy, and discussing US-China fiscal issues and economic reform.[21]

Projecting power means that China should be seen as a capable stakeholder in the system, willing to invest in countries suffering from or vulnerable to conflict (read: Africa), and to strengthen institutions in which China is willing to invest and for which it possesses the resources. It implies that China is developing an image based on the idea that Chinese power is not as it was understood historically (based on a tributary system where countries would have to pay tribute to China and accept its power based on coercion and force). Instead, what China is attempting to do is to bring about a sense of legitimacy by showcasing its power through regional institutional mechanisms, broadcasting its economic power and economic largeness, as well as shoring up its military presence. It is aggressively exploring avenues of resources in and around its own coastline, which is bringing it into conflict with its neighbors. Nevertheless, broadcasting power is accomplished by asserting claims on territory that were once seen as Chinese but were lost due to the events of history—for instance, the events of the late 19th century to about 1949, which are termed the "Century of Humiliation" in China. As a result, expressing claims on territory, backing it up by a show of force, and physically challenging others are parts of the power-backed demonstration package. This aspect was witnessed in 2012 when China published a map in its E-passport that showed islands in East and South China Seas along with Arunachal Pradesh and Aksai Chin in India over which it has staked its claims since the 1940s as Chinese territories.[22] While there are claims that Chinese strategic culture is defensive, perhaps since the time of Sun Tzu's *Art of War*, this has been refuted by Iain Johnston, who has defined strategic culture as "ranked grand strategic preferences derived from central paradigmatic assumptions about the nature of conflict and the enemy, and collectively shared by decision makers."[23] Johnston carried out a close and detailed assessment of the Seven Military Classics of ancient China and concluded that there was a Confucian/Mencian-dominated set of assumptions that viewed diplomacy and economic incentives as merely

---

[21] "China, US Argue Economic Reform at G20 Meeting," Peoples' Daily, February 26, 2014, <http://english.people.com.cn/98649/8546831.html>.

[22] "China Shows Arunachal Pradesh and Aksai Chin as its Territory," Indian Express, November 23, 2012, <http://archive.indianexpress.com/news/china-shows-arunachal-pradesh-and-aksai-chin-as-its-territory/1035332/>.

[23] Warren I. Cohen, "China's Strategic Culture," The Atlantic, March 1997, <https://www.theatlantic.com/past/docs/issues/97mar/china/china.htm>.

symbolic gestures, but the best way to deal with a threat to China was with the use of force and strategy. According to Johnston, the Chinese classics stressed the role of violence-based solutions to conflicts. Nonviolent means were only seen as particularly expedient when one was facing a powerful adversary; hence, negotiation and diplomacy were seen as delaying tactics. Therefore, for China to argue that it has a pacifist culture and history is not supported by its past writings and strategic thinking.

Interestingly, the Seven Military Classics were widely read by Ming Dynasty emperors, the scholarly officials, and so on. What is even more telling is that between 1950 and 1985, there were eleven foreign policy crises in eight of which China resorted to violence. It can be inferred from historical texts and China's strategic behavior that China is more likely to use force in a historical dispute, especially one connected to a historically sensitive issue and territory. China's posture towards Taiwan and Tibet and its use of force against India over Aksai Chin and Arunachal Pradesh (then North East Frontier Agency) in 1962, which led to India's devastating defeat, vindicates this assertion. Even earlier, in 1950, Mao Tse Tung led a confrontation with the United States in the Korean peninsula. As a result of the enduring influence of Chinese strategic culture, which considers the use of force a viable mechanism against threats to Chinese territory or in order to broadcast one's own power, it is unlikely that a new generation of Chinese leaders will forgo ancient thinking on strategy that has held them in good stead. Therefore, China is going to be serious about power projection, and negotiations will be utilized only in the context of tremendous power disparity where China is the weaker actor.[24] This style of strategy and negotiation will not change even when there is generational change in the CCP or with the coming of new leadership, as it is time-tested and has worked in China's favor. However, this belief in force and military power will be mitigated to a large extent by China's desire to rise in a manner that does not unravel the international architecture from which it has benefitted and of which it is an integral part. What it would try to accomplish is more wiggle room and space in international forums, establishing itself as the major power in international politics.

---

[24] Ibid.

India's Power Projection and Role

India has emerged as a powerful Asian country, important enough to play a decisive role in Asian geopolitics. With its economic growth making it the third largest economy in the world[25] after the US and China, India can shape world events and credibly pledge resources to better regional institutional infrastructure. It has been playing a major role in regional institutions like the South Asian Association for Regional Cooperation (SAARC), its centrality being reflected when heads of states of the SAARC nations including the Prime Minister of Mauritius participated in Indian Prime Minister Narendra Modi's swearing-in at the latter's invitation in 2014.[26] This was the first time that SAARC countries' heads of state and government were invited for an Indian Prime Minister's oath-taking ceremony, and it represents a symbolic acceptance of India's desire to include its neighbors in its own path to prosperity and greatness. Critically, the acceptance of the invitation by Pakistan Prime Minister Nawaz Sharif is symbolically significant, given the fact that India-Pakistan relations have not been some of the best considering their history of wars, presence of nuclear weapons, and cross-border terror activities.

In this context, there are three strategic pillars that have impacted India's strategic choices and preferences:

1. Improving bilateral relationship with the US; effect on China
2. Rise of China and India's Response
3. Indian Strategic Culture

---

[25] "India becomes World's Third Largest Economy," Al Jazeera, April 30, 2014, <http://www.aljazeera.com/news/asia/2014/04/india-becomes-world-third-largest-economy-20144301534534 23300.html>.

[26] Mayank Aggrawal, "Narendra Modi's Swearing-In: SAARC Makes History, Comes Together for a New Experience," DNA Analysis, May 27, 2014, <http://www.dnaindia.com/india/report-narendra-modi-s-swearing-in-saarc-makes-history-comes-together-for-a-new-experience-1991566>.

Improving Bilateral Relationship with the US; Effect on China

Significantly and in a major strategic gesture, India signed a civilian nuclear deal with the US in July 2005, signaling a *de facto* recognition of India as a nuclear weapons state. In relation to its immediate neighborhood, India has maintained sustained influence in South Asia and has sought to counterbalance Chinese inroads on its borders in Northeast India by linking its strategic interests with the US. India faces vulnerable neighbors, unlike China with its economically vibrant ones, and therefore has a harder task.[27] Given India's growing regional clout and global ambitions,[28] the US is looking towards India for a larger role in regional and global security matters. In the January 2012 Department of Defense (DoD) guideline document titled "Sustaining U.S. Global Leadership: Priorities for 21st Century Defense," India was recognized as a strategic partner with the US for maintaining regional peace and security, especially in the Indian Ocean.[29] China has, however, viewed this growing India-US bilateral relationship with suspicion, interpreting it as a "containment of China" policy. Disturbingly for India, a sudden shift in China's behavior with regard to Arunachal Pradesh was discernible in 2006 after the 2005 India-US nuclear deal. In November 2006, just days before Chinese Premier Hu Jintao's state visit to India, Chinese Ambassador to India Sun Yuxi stated that "[i]n our position, the whole of the state of Arunachal Pradesh is Chinese territory. And Tawang is only one of the places in it. We are claiming all of that. That is our position".[30] In May 2007, China denied a visa to Ganesh Koyu, the Indian Administrative Service (IAS) Officer from Arunachal Pradesh and in 2009 blocked India's request for a loan from the ADB.[31]

---

[27] See C. Rajamohan, "India and the Balance of Power," Foreign Affairs, July-August 2006, <http://www.foreignaffairs.org/20060701faessay85402/c-raja-mohan/india-and-the-balance-of-power.html>.

[28] Namrata Goswami, "Foreign Policy Priorities for India 2014," Foreign Policy Journal, May 26, 2014, <http://www.foreignpolicyjournal.com/2014/05/26/foreign-policy-priorities-for-india-2014/#.U4RKmXKSyxo>.

[29] Department of Defense, "Sustaining U.S. Global Leadership: Priorities for 21st Century Defense," January 2012, <http://www.defense.gov/news/Defense_Strategic_Guidance.pdf>.

[30] "Arunachal Pradesh is our Territory: Chinese Envoy," November 14, 2006, <http://www.rediff.com/news/2006/nov/14china.htm>.

[31] Sudha Ramachandran, "Chinese Antics have India Fuming," Asia Times, May 05, 2009, <http://www.atimes.com/atimes/South_Asia/KE05Df01.html>.

Why this sudden assertive Chinese posture against India despite having a mechanism for talks on territorial disputes through the "Special Representatives" platform and the 2014 Border Defense Cooperation Agreement (BDCA)? In terms of balance of power, the timing and the context is significant. China is wary of the growing India-US strategic partnership since the end of the Cold War and further cemented by the Indo-US Civil Nuclear Deal of July 18, 2005.[32] This was subsequently followed by the signing of the India-US Civil Nuclear Cooperation Agreement on October 8, 2008.[33] This agreement was further vindicated by President Obama's rather successful visit to India in January 2015 to attend India's Republic day.[34] Earlier, in 2004, India and the US had signed the "Next Steps in Strategic Partnership (NSSP)," which outlined intensive cooperation in civilian nuclear activities, civilian space programs, and high-technology trade, and expanded dialogue on missile defense through a series of reciprocal steps.[35] This got renewed for another ten years in January 2015. Moreover, the US and India signed for the first time a joint strategic vision for the Asia Pacific in which the freedom of navigation, especially in the South China Sea, found special mention.[36]

China interprets the strengthening India-US relations as being motivated by one over-arching paradigm: containing China.[37] To Chinese observers, the US is propping up India as a hedge against China.[38] In fact, Chinese

---

[32] "Indo-US Joint Statement," July 18, 2005,
<http://www.hindu.com/thehindu/nic/indousjoint.htm>.
[33] "India, United States Sign Historic Civil Nuclear Agreement,"India Review, Embassy of India, Washington D.C., November 1, 2008, 1-24.
[34] "U.S.-India Joint Statement साँझा प्रयास - सबका विकास" – "Shared Effort; Progress for All," The White House, January 25, 2015, <http://www.whitehouse.gov/the-press-office/2015/01/25/us-india-joint-statement-shared-effort-progress-all>.
[35] "Joint Press Statement: Next Steps in Strategic Partnership between India and the United States," Embassy of India, Washington D.C., September 17, 2004,
<http://www.indianembassy.org/prdetail1148/joint-press-statement-%3A-next-steps-in-strategic-partnership-between-india-and-the-united-states>.
[36] "U.S.-India Joint Strategic Vision for the Asia Pacific and Indian Ocean Region," The White House, January 25, 2015,
<http://www.whitehouse.gov/the-press-office/2015/01/25/us-india-joint-strategic-vision-asia-pacific-and-indian-ocean-region>.
[37] George Perkovich, "Faulty Promises. The U.S.-India Nuclear Deal," Carnegie Endowment for International Peace, September 2005, 1-14.
[38] See Jeff M. Smith, "India as a US hedge against China," Asia Times, August 07, 2008, <http://www.atimes.com/atimes/South_Asia/JH07Df01.html>. Also see: Ehsan Ahrari, "China's View of US 'lily pad' Strategy," Asia Times, August 24, 2004,

commentators interpreted the recent Obama-Modi photogenic moments as mere show with little substance to demonstrate and perhaps brought together by their common desire to limit China's growth and influence. The China National Radio asserted that "[t]he US wants to use India to contain China, but Delhi may not agree to such a strategy. Instead, commercial benefits and military technology are the things that India is hoping to gain from the US."[39]

This interpretation that India is covertly joining a Western bandwagon to contain China is not new. In 2009, two important Chinese blogs[40] argued that India's dispatch of an additional 60,000 forces to Arunachal Pradesh was part of a covert Western plan to contain China.[41] The Chinese claim on Arunachal Pradesh was therefore maintained as a bargaining chip. The Chinese blogs viewed the Chinese military exercise held at Chengdu in 2009 as a fitting counter to India-US partnership. China's border forces were stationed at Rikaze and east of Yadong, and a new airport was constructed at Ali with 4500-meter long runway capable of launching fighters and bombers. The *Global Times,* the English edition of the *People's Daily* (published since April 20, 2009) in an editorial on June 11, 2009 categorically asserted that Arunachal Pradesh is "southern Tibet" and part of China. It interpreted the 60,000 Indian troops on the international border as an expression of India's fear and frustration at China's rise, since India cannot hope to match China in international influence, national power, and economic scale. India, the editorial argued, should give up "wishful thinking" that China would make compromises on territory. [42] According to a BBC survey of global opinion[43], 47% of Chinese viewed India as a "dirty, third rate sort of place."[44]

        <http://www.atimes.com/atimes/China/FH24Ad04.html>.

[39] "China Media: India-US Ties 'Superficial,'" BBC, January 26, 2015, <http://www.bbc.com/news/world-asia-china-30978185>.

[40] See: <www.junshi315.cn> and <www.warchina.com/n8183c21.aspx>, December 11, 2009, analyzed by D.S. Rajan, "China: Nationalistic Blogs Raise New Issues Concerning Sino- Indian Border," South Asia Analysis Group, Paper no. 3562, 24-Dec-2009, <http://www.southasiaanalysis.org/%5Cpapers36%5Cpaper3562.html>.

[41] Incidentally, estimated Indian troops presence in Arunachal Pradesh is about 120,000. Field observations by the author in Arunachal Pradesh in March 2011.

[42] B. Raman, "Chinese Media Fury over Arunachal Pradesh," South Asia Analysis Group, Paper no.3251, June 12, 2009,
<http://www.southasiaanalysis.org/%5Cpapers33%5Cpaper3251.html>.

[43] See: "BBC World Service Poll," <http://news.bbc.co.uk/2/shared/bsp/hi/pdfs/160410bbcwspoll.pdf>. 38% of Indians view China negatively.

[44] See: The Economist, "A Himalayan Rivalry," n. 8.

Ironically, the current situation between India and China reveals a classic "prisoner's dilemma," where two actors are aware of neither each other's intentions nor capabilities and hence inadvertently indulge in action that could prove counter-productive in the end. In 2011, a publication in the People's Liberation Army's official newspaper, *PLA Daily*, stated that India's bold military moves in the eastern sector are motivated by a desire to "contain China" since India views China as a *de facto* competitor in Asia. The *PLA Daily* article further argued that in alliance with the West (read: the US), India aims to balance China by carrying out its largest military upgrade since 1962 in the eastern sector.[45]

The Chinese strategic logic of balancing in Arunachal Pradesh is also informed by the continuing "security dilemma"[46] in India-China relations. This "security dilemma" arises as China seeks to establish closer ties with countries in South Asia/Indian Ocean region, and India is wary of such links.[47] China has always followed a "balance of power" approach to counter India. Besides trying to establish itself in South Asia by forging closer ties with Bangladesh, Nepal, and Sri Lanka, China has, both covertly and overtly, assisted Pakistan's nuclear and missile efforts, its military and military-industrial capabilities.[48] The fundamental core of China-Pakistan relations is the "balance of power" logic *vis-à-vis* India. China's behavior with Pakistan indicates a belief within the Chinese decision-making circle that an adversarial relation between India and Pakistan will negate India's ambition for major power status in Asia. Also, the mere existence of the Pakistani threat in India's western sector limits India's military capability *vis-à-vis* China in the eastern sector and strengthens China's ability to realize its territorial

---

[45] Namrata Goswami, "China's Response to India's Military Upgrade in Arunachal Pradesh: A Classic Case of 'Security Dilemma,'" IDSA Strategic Comment, November 18, 2011,
<http://www.idsa.in/idsacomments/ChinasResponsetoIndiasMilitaryUpgradeinArunachalPradesh_ngoswami_181111>.

[46] For more on this, see: John Garver, "The security dilemma in Sino-Indian relations," India Review, 1/4, 2002, 1-38. Security dilemma "arises out of the anarchic nature of the state system. Without a superior power to protect it, each state bears the ultimate responsibility for its own security, for its own survival as a member of the state system. Faced with awesome responsibility, states attempt to expand their power—economically, strategically, and militarily—so as to defend themselves." This makes neighboring states insecure and hence they prepare for the worst by taking counter-measures to enhance their own power. A common search for security results in a situation in which both powers are less secure. Garver, 1.

[47] Ibid., 3-4.

[48] Ibid, 4. Also see: "Contest of the Century," The Economist, n.46.

claims. For China, the two front war situations for India, coupled with the memory of China's 1962 defeat of India, guards against any Indian ambition to counter China in Asia. Hence, Chinese policymakers engage in aggressive territorial posturing in Arunachal Pradesh to keep Indian ambitions in check.[49]

Internal debates within China have revealed the view that China should teach India a lesson with regard to Arunachal Pradesh. This would assure China's superiority in the regional military balance and teach the US a lesson for cultivating India against China.[50] According to the *Chinese White Paper on Defense 2010*, China aims to win local wars by using information techniques based on the concept of jointness.[51] Given that China is wary of India's desire to become a military power in the South Asia/Indian Ocean region[52], it has upgraded the infrastructure near the international border in Arunachal Pradesh by building an extensive network of roads, railheads, forward airfields, pipelines, and logistic hubs for supporting military operations. China has deployed intercontinental missiles such as the DF-31 and DF-31A at Delingha, north of Tibet. On the border itself, China has deployed "13 Border Defence Regiments, the 52nd Mountain Infantry Brigade to protect Southern Qinghai-Tibet region, the 53rd Mountain Infantry Brigade to protect the high plateau in the Western sector, the 149th Division of the 13th Group Army in the eastern sector and the 61st Division of the 21st Group Army in the western sector."[53] Airfields have been established at Hoping, Pangta, and Kong Ka,

---

[49] Garver, n. 51, 9. See: SIPRI Yearbooks 1981-2009 for Chinese Arms Transfers to Pakistan, <http://www.sipri.org/databases>.

[50] See: <www.warchina.com/n88582c21.aspx>, December 1, 2009, and <www.warchina.com/n8183c21.aspx>, December 9, 2009, analyzed by D. S. Rajan, "China: Nationalistic Blogs Raise New Issues Concerning Sino- Indian Border," South Asia Analysis Group, Paper no. 3562, 24-Dec-2009, <http://www.southasiaanalysis.org/%5Cpapers36%5Cpaper3562.html>.

[51] "China's National Defense in 2010," Information Office of the State Council, Peoples' Republic of China, March 2011, <http://news.xinhuanet.com/english2010/china/2011-03/31/c_13806851.htm>. Informatization "emphasizes the effects of modern information technology on military decisions and weapons employment cycles." See: Department of Defense Report, US, n.5, 3.

[52] D.S. Rajan, "How China views India's new defence doctrine," January 07, 2010, <http://news.rediff.com/column/2010/jan/07/how-china-views-indias-new-defence-doctrine.htm>.

[53] Vijay Sakhuja, "Military Buildup Across the Himalayas: A Shaky Balance," China Brief, 9/18, September 10, 2009, <http://www.jamestown.org/programs/chinabrief/single/?tx_ttnews%5Btt_news%5D=35469&tx_ttnews%5BbackPid%5D=25&cHash=255e0ccfe7>. "Military and Security Developments Involving the People's Republic of China 2010," US Department of Defense, 2010, <http://www.defense.gov/pubs/pdfs/2010_CMPR_Final.pdf>.

along with two airfields at Lhasa and an additional four in the region to support fighter aircraft and enhance the PLA's airlift capability, which includes a division of troops (20,000), a brigade of air-drops (3,500 troops) and helicopter lift capability for two battalions.[54] The 2010 US Department of Defense Report to Congress states that China has replaced its old liquid-fueled, nuclear-capable CSS-3 inter-mediate range ballistic missile with "more advanced CSS-5 MRBMs" and has vastly improved its border roads in the eastern sector bordering India for PLA movement.[55]

Rise of China and India's Response

India has been quite open with its China policy by aiming to build new strategic roadways in its eastern sector, especially in Arunachal Pradesh. It declared 2006 as the India-China friendship year, and 2007 was declared the India-China year of tourism.[56] Yet when it comes to Indian-Chinese political relations, the balancing of convergent interests can sometimes get tricky. As mentioned earlier, China's territorial claims on Indian territory complicate the relationship. Since July 1, 2006, India has had voiced concerns over Chinese road/train linkages from Qinghai leading right up to Lhasa and its plans to build roads to the border of Nepal. Chinese road-building and military modernization[57] have made India uneasy and have led to India's forces in the eastern sector being augmented. After the U.S. declared India a responsible nuclear power with advanced nuclear technology, China may have hoped to tip India's balance by creating problems in its eastern sector concerning Arunachal Pradesh.[58] When one reviews India's grand strategic thoughts, what emerges is that the realist school of thought in India, as well as those studying power transitions, argue that states in an anarchic international

---

[54] Ibid.
[55] Department of Defense Report, US, n.50, 38.
[56] Surjit Mansingh, "Rising China and Emergent India in the 21st Century: Friends or Rivals?" The Korean Journal of Defence Analysis, XIX/4, Winter, 2007, 117-142.
[57] See David Shambaugh, "China Military Modernization: Making Steady and Surprising Progress," in Ashley Tellis and Michael Wills (ed.), *Military Modernization in an Era*, Seattle: The National Bureau of Asian Research, 2005. Also see: Namrata Goswami, "China's Territorial Claim on Arunachal Pradesh: Alternative Scenarios 2032," IDSA Occasional Paper. No. 29, November 2012, 1-47.
[58] See India-U.S. Statement of 18 July 2005,
<http://www.indianembassy.org/press_release/2005/July/21.htm>.

order have to take care of themselves. Moreover, interest, power, and violence are intrinsic to international politics. Therefore, India must rise to the reality of threat and counter-threat with regards to China.[59] The lack of a supranational authority forestalls the tragedy of balance of power, deterrence, and war. The only way to secure oneself, therefore, is accumulation of military power and use of force. Realists would argue against the possibilities of institutional cooperation and economic exchange mitigating Indian-Chinese differences. The only way to do so is through nuclear deterrence and military means. It must therefore try to encircle China by building alliances, most notably with the US.[60] Realists support strengthened Indian relations with Vietnam, Burma, Taiwan, Japan, South Korea, and the ASEAN states as a balancer to the rise of China. Realists desire a strong Indian naval presence in the South and East China Seas.

This realist strategy has been witnessed on the ground in East and Southeast Asia. A three-year agreement on oil and natural gas exploration in the South China Sea was signed in October 2011 between India's state-run Oil and Natural Gas Corporation (ONGC) Videsh and Vietnam's PetroVietnam. In response, China's Foreign Ministry spokesperson Jiang Yu stated that "our consistent position is that we are opposed to any country engaging in oil and gas exploration and development activities in waters under Chinese jurisdiction." She went on to stress that China enjoyed "indisputable sovereignty" over the South China Sea and its islands. In fact, China's assertiveness with regard to the South China Sea was evident when it radioed an Indian Navy ship *INS Airavat* in July 2012 to leave "Chinese waters" while the ship was making a trip in international waters near the South China Sea.[61]

In response to this, India raised the ante by signing defense deals and establishing naval cooperation with countries such as Vietnam, South Korea, Japan, and Australia, especially to guarantee "freedom of navigation" in international waters. To be sure, India views China's recent assertiveness in India's eastern sector and the South China Sea as a display of Chinese

---

[59] Bharat Karnad (ed.), *Future Imperiled: India's Security in the 1990s and Beyond* (New Delhi: Viking, 1990). Also Brahma Chellany (ed.), *Securing India's Future in the New Millennium* (New Delhi: Orient Longman and Centre for Policy Research, 1999).

[60] Bharat Karnad, *Nuclear Weapons and Indian Security: The Realist Foundations of Strategy* (New Delhi: Macmillan, 2002), 557-612.

[61] "China Warship Warns Indian Navy Vessel in South China Sea," The Economic Times, September 01, 2011, <http://articles.economictimes.indiatimes.com/2011-09-01/news/29953708_1_ins-airavat-south-china-sea-chinese-navy>.

power: a desire to maximize its share of world power, which means gaining power at the expense of other states in the system. Consequently, former Indian Prime Minister Manmohan Singh and Vietnamese President Truong Tan Sang jointly committed to securing vital sea lanes of communication (SLOCs) (read: South China Sea) during Sang's visit to India in October 2011.[62] Vietnam's Deputy Chief of General Staff, Lieutenant General Pham Xuan Hung, visited India in December 2011 and held talks with India's then-Chief of Naval Staff, Admiral Navin Kumar Verma, and then-Chief of the Indian Army, General V. K. Singh.[63] Most significantly, Vietnam has already accorded India the right to use its Nha Trang Port on the Western shore of the South China Sea.

India decided to boost defense cooperation with Japan during the visit of its former Defense Minister, A. K. Antony, to Tokyo in November 2011; ensuring the security of SLOCs was paramount in this visit.[64] In 2012, Japan and India held the Japan-India Defense Policy Dialogue in Tokyo, in which the Japanese and Indian militaries participated in joint exercises. While joint naval exercises had been held in the past, this was the first time that the air forces of both countries held exercises.[65] Japan is already an integral part of the multi-lateral Malabar Naval Exercise in the Indian Ocean region between India, the US, Australia, and Singapore. Prime Minister Narendra Modi visited Japan in September 2014 and signed pacts with his Japanese counterpart, Shinzo Abe, with regards to defense and strategic cooperation and ensuring freedom of navigation.

The most critical development between India and Japan was the first ever "Trilateral Dialogue," held on December 19, 2011 in Washington D.C. between India, Japan, and the US to discuss a range of issues concerning

---

[62] "India, Vietnam join hands for oil exploration in S China Sea," The Hindu Business Line, October 12, 2011, <http://www.thehindubusinessline.com/industry-and-economy/article2531334.ece>.

[63] "Vietnam General Staff Delegation Visits India," Tuoitrenews News, 4 December 2011, <http://www.tuoitrenews.vn/cmlink/tuoitrenews/politics/vietnam-general-staff-delegation-visits-india-1.53459>.

[64] K. V. Prasad, "India, Japan to Step up Defence Cooperation," The Hindu, 3 November 2011, <http://www.thehindu.com/news/international/article2593792.ece>.

[65] "Maritime Security Issues Dominate India-Japan Defence talks, India and Japan to step up Bilateral Military Exercises, India-Japan Defence Cooperation 'Geared' towards Peace and Prosperity —Antony," Press Information Bureau, Government of India, 3 November 2011, <http://pib.nic.in/newsite/erelease.aspx?relid=76976>. Also see: Sandeep Dikshit, "India, Japan to Hold Second 2+2 Dialogue on Monday," The Hindu, 18 October 2012.

the Asia Pacific.⁶⁶ This was a significant development for three specific reasons. Firstly, it involves India, an Indian Ocean country, in Pacific affairs for the first time. Secondly, it indicates that concern over China's assertiveness in the Asia Pacific is growing among the democracies in the region. Thirdly, it signals a shift in India's policy from being wary of US influence in Asia to directly engaging it in the format of a dialogue concerning Asia-Pacific issues.

To further cement that policy shift, India signed a five-year defense cooperation agreement with another East Asian country and a traditional US ally, South Korea, to enhance the strategic partnership between them. This occurred during the visit of former Indian defense minister, A. K. Antony, to South Korea in September 2010.⁶⁷ The strategic partnership envisioned exchange of military personnel, exchange visits of ships and aircrafts, and ensuring the safety of the SLOCs. Significantly, in December 2011, India and Australia committed themselves to "freedom of navigation" in international waters during the visit of the Australian defense minister, Stephen Smith, to India. Joint military exercises have been envisioned as well. In fact, the deepening Indian-Australian relations could be discerned from the fact that Australia briefed India on the US plans to station 2,500 Marines in Darwin, Australia as part of the US policy to re-engage in Asia.⁶⁸ All these strategic partnerships established by India with Japan, South Korea, Vietnam, and Australia clearly indicate, from a realist perspective, a balancing strategy towards China in East Asia.

India's Strategic Culture and Preferences

There has been enormous debate on what India's strategic culture is; the general impression in strategic circles is that India lacks a strategic culture. This was articulated in the much quoted and studied essay by George K.

---

[66] Josh Rogin, "Inside the First Ever U.S.-Japan-India Trilateral Meeting," Foreign Policy, 23 December 2011,
<http://thecable.foreignpolicy.com/posts/2011/12/23/inside_the_first_ever_us_japan_india_trilateral_meeting>.

[67] Rajeev Sharma, "A. K. Antony's Seoul Mission," The Diplomat, 1 September 2010, <http://thediplomat.com/indian-decade/2010/09/01/a-k-antonys-seoul-mission/>.

[68] "India-Australia Discuss Military Ties," ABC News, 8 December 2011, <http://www.abc.net.au/news/2011-12-08/india-and-australia-discuss-military-ties/3719190>.

Tanham, "Indian Strategic Thought. An Interpretive Essay,"[69] which faults India for lacking a strategic culture by which mechanisms of progress and change are individually orchestrated and engineered, and in the recent articles from *The Economist* lamenting how the absence of Indian strategic thinking downgrades India's stature as a major power in the world.[70] However, the limitation of these arguments is that they mistake India's desire to chalk a path for itself, devoid of cozying up to military alliances like NATO or American led alliances, as a lack of strategic culture. Significantly, strategic culture is how elites perceive threats and opportunities and the means that they would support to forward a particular end goal. There are broad preferences within the Indian strategic community across regional divides on the efficacy and usefulness of the use of force to forward foreign policy goals.

In order to understand what Indian strategic culture is, there are, broadly, two major interpretations. One is what I call "hardcore realism," for which the projection of military power beyond India's borders will improve India's international influence and secure its borders *vis-a-vis* China and Pakistan. Realists view the instability in Pakistan, the rising power of China, and the unresolved border issue as serious external threats mitigated by broadcasting efficient and effective military power at the border with Pakistan and China, and projecting Indian naval power in the Indian Ocean. Realists support increased defense spending, which by *The Economist*'s own admission poises India to become the fourth largest military power in the world by 2020.

The other ideational base of Indian strategic culture is the Nehruvian (fashioned after Jawaharlal Nehru, India's first Prime Minister) commitment to use military power only as a last resort, not until the last diplomatic note has been written. Nehruvians firmly believe that dialogue rather than military force is the best way to resolve conflicts with either Pakistan or China. They have faith in the ability of international organizations to mitigate international conflict and are wary of security alliances apart from the UN. Nehruvians are against India joining security alliances of any nature that could potentially

---

[69] George K. Tanham, "Indian Strategic Thought: An Interpretive Essay," (RAND: Santa Monica: 1992).

[70] "India as a Great Power Know Your Strength," The Economist, March 30, 2013, <http://www.economist.com/news/briefing/21574458-india-poised-become-one-four-largest-military-powers-world-end>. "Can India become a Great Power?" The Economist, March 30, 2013, <http://www.economist.com/news/leaders/21574511-indias-lack-strategic-culture-hobbles-its-ambition-be-force-world-can-india>.

create conflicts and undermine world peace. Military power projection, for them, is purely reserved for an act of self-defense as defined by Article 51 of the UN Charter. Aligning with other states for the purpose of a common broadcasting of military strength is not supported by Nehruvians, hence their commitment to non-alignment and aversion to militarized western security groupings.

Interestingly, India's Nehruvian strategic thought falls in the category of liberal institutionalism. Despite believing in the anarchic nature of international politics, adherents of this school accept the proposition that international law, institutions, military restraint, negotiations, cooperation, and free communication would mitigate conflicts. They argue that balance of power and war preparedness are futile, as they lead to the very conditions they aim to address, namely insecurity and conflict.[71] With regard to the rise of China, Nehruvians argue that China is not an imperial power and that it is trying to come to terms with its hundred years of occupation in the 19th century following the Opium Wars. They believe that China's desire to reunify Taiwan is justified, as it originally belonged to China. Given the fact that its Communist regime has been able to uplift the Chinese people and elevate China to a great power status, China must be given its due share in the international order. With regard to Indian-Chinese relations, Nehruvians argue that other areas of interaction must not be held hostage to the border issue. They state that since China and India do not have historical enmity and are two great civilizations, there are many grounds for convergence.

Of note is the fact that trade between India and China increased considerably to US $75.45 billion in 2011 but fell to US $65 billion in 2013, with a growing trade deficit of 31.4% for India, resulting in a slowdown of trade.[72] Despite this, both countries have a common interest in keeping Asia free of conflict. What can be inferred from several official pronouncements is that India aims to build a stable and prosperous Asia in concert with China and other major

---

[71] Kanti P. Bajpai, "Pakistan and China in Indian Strategic Thought," International Journal, August 2007, 805-22.
[72] "India-China Trade Expected to Touch $ 100 billion by 2015," The Economic Times, 26 October 26 2012, <http://articles.economictimes.indiatimes.com/2012-10-26/news/34750100_1_india-china-trade-china-international-auto-parts-bilateral-trade>. Also see: Ananth Krishnan, "India-China Trade: Record $ 31 bn Deficit in 2013," The Hindu, January 10, 2014, <http://www.thehindu.com/business/indiachina-trade-record-31-bn-deficit-in-2013/article5562569.ece>.

Asian countries and to ensure that they do not come into mutual conflict. With regard to ASEAN institutional convergence, New Delhi has signed a number of economic and military agreements with the organization. India is an observer in the SCO and a partner in the East Asian Summit and the African Union. The liberals argue that now, with the signing of a Free Trade Agreement with ASEAN,[73] regional cooperation will only contribute to mitigating tensions in Asia.

The key question that confronts us now is whether the strategic choices and preferences and the geopolitical environment within which China and India find themselves will over-shadow the West's long dominance of the international system. For reasons of strategic consequence, the critical puzzle is whether the rise of China and India as major powers will propel them to shape their own strategic choices and preferences in such a way that it brings them into conflict with the Western, American-led conception of the international system.

One factor that may bring about conflict is China's enormous thirst for resources and its plans to cultivate relationships with countries in Africa and Latin America for this purpose.[74] It is vital that rising powers do not view the current international system as sub-optimal for their own development and quest for power and prestige due to its implicit favor for current great powers. Rising powers must be assisted in cultivating stakes in the present order as well as in understanding the interdependent nature of international politics, where no single country can rise on its own and hope to develop itself internally or sustain a level of growth without external cooperation. The current international system should develop receptive radars to the preferences of China and India, as dissatisfaction with international structures and processes on their part could generate revisionary tendencies. It is critical that countries like the US, the lead shaper of international institutions and practices, understand the reasons behind military modernization, especially in China. It is mostly a response to the security dilemma existing in East Asia, where China perceives a threat to itself and its historical claims on islands and Taiwan from the US's presence as well as

---

[73] "India, ASEAN Finalise on FTA in Services and Investments," The Hindu, 21 December 2012, <http://www.thehindu.com/todays-paper/tp-business/india-asean-finalise-fta-in-services-and-investments/article4224026.ece>.

[74] Rahim Kanani, "By All Means Necessary: How China's Resource Quest Is Changing The World," Forbes, April 15, 2014, <http://www.forbes.com/fdc/welcome_mjx.shtml>.

from the security alliances between the US, Japan, and the Philippines.[75] Despite this, the intriguing and major trend is China's increasing role in international institutions, formulating international norms, and having visible hesitation in challenging international rules. Yet if one notices Chinese behavior, it has especially engaged with those states that the Western-led international system set aside for special sanctions or international isolation, namely Myanmar during the reign of the military junta, Sudan, North Korea, and Zimbabwe—states that were/are seen as rogues.

Yet another critical development that has brought about a shift in real power are the levels of military expenditure. While the US still far outnumbers the rest of the world in terms of defense expenditure, according to SIPRI estimates there has been a shift from 2012 onwards of defense expenditures from the West to the East. While it is true that US expenditure fell by 6% in 2012, it was still 69% higher than in 2001 when defense expenditure went up tremendously after the 9/11 attacks. One can explain this shift in US defense expenditure by the overall reduction in all US government budgets following the 2008 US financial crisis, particularly the reduction in money allocated to Overseas Contingency Operations (OCOs) in Afghanistan and Iraq from US $159 billion in 2011 to US $115 billion in 2012. This change was brought about by the Budget Control Act of 2011. In fact, the US will reduce its defense expenditure by US $55 billion each year from 2013 to 2021. In this comparative context, China's military expenditure has been the highest in Asia, rising by 175% from 2003 to 2012. To be noted is the fact that expenditures in Vietnam and Indonesia have gone up, especially in their naval capacity. This is primarily propelled by perceived threats in the South China Seas, and, for India, perceived aggressiveness from China on their common border has made a case for greater allocation of funds for defense.[76] In 2013, Asia's military spending also rose, with US $322 billion spent on military budgets, up from US $262 billion in 2010.[77]

The security dilemma aspect has played out in East Asia as is seen from the increasing defense expenditure in South Korea with its acquisition of the

---

[75] Scott L. Kastner and Phillip C. Saunders, "Is China a Status Quo or Revisionist State? Leadership Travel as an Empirical Indicator of Foreign Policy Priorities," International Studies Quarterly, 56, 2012, 164.

[76] Sam Perlo-Freeman, et.al., "Trends in World Military Expenditure, 2012", SIPRI FACT Sheet, April 2013, 2-6.

[77] Carola Hoyos, "Asian Military Spending on the Rise," Financial Times, April 21, 2014, <http://www.ft.com/intl/cms/s/0/af1000e8-8e89-11e3-98c6-00144feab7de.html#axzz30AaVKOsq>.

Medium Multi-Role Combat Aircraft (MMRCA), Japan's purchase of the F-35, as well as increases in per-soldier allocation of resources. It is also important to note that countries like China, India, Japan, and South Korea were putting less stress on imported weapons systems in order to become self-reliant in arms production.[78] This thrust for indigenization has been termed as techno-nationalism; whereas developed countries pursued global supply chains of arms production, Asia was persistent in its techno-nationalist approach of self-sufficiency, sometimes at high costs. This kind of indigenization is dependent on localized Research & Development (R&D) to support new technology. India has its HF-Marut from the 1960s, the state-owned and -run Defense Research & Development Organization (DRDO), including eight public sector undertakings and 40 ordnance factories. Japan has its Mitsubishi Heavy Industries, Mitsubishi Electric, Kawasaki Heavy Industries, etc.[79] This kind of focus on arms manufacturing and procurement with the heady mix of nationalism and territorial conflicts makes East Asia a region perhaps "ripe for rivalry."[80] Yet optimism is also present, especially for those who believe that mutual interdependence has increased prospects of mutual governance and cooperation.[81]

As a result, one can conclude neither that geopolitics or geography will bring about alignments based on *West versus East*, nor that China or India's strategic preferences and choices will overshadow that of the West. Instead, there will be competing claims for legitimacy and relevance within Asia over the ideational influences of pluralistic underpinnings of Indian democracy and the authoritarian single-mindedness of China. There will be no common Asian alliance against the West but rather alliances and partnerships based on common interest and threat perceptions. Hence, one cannot merrily ride the imaginary wave that geopolitics will bring Asia into one cohesive whole

---

[78] Chien-pin Li, "Fear, Greed, or Garage Sale? The Analysis of Military Expenditure in East Asia", The Pacific Review, 10/2, 1997, 426.
[79] Ibid., 431.
[80] Ibid., 274.
[81] Ibid., 275.

while forgetting that some of the countries have major alliances/security partnerships with the West that have worked to their benefit. However, there will be a natural resistance to overt American influence, be it in China's sphere of historical influence or for India in South Asia. While China and India will compete over who is the natural leader of Asia, they will sometimes join hands in a fight against Western imposition, based on and propelled by their own strategic preferences. Yet these strategic preferences will not be exclusive to the West but will be determined by the exigencies of time and space, and will at times be aligned with the interests of Western powers.

Indian soldiers in a trench, World War I

China's Choice: Contributing to the Emergence of a Concert of Powers in the Asia-Pacific

Pang Zhongying

"Among the lessons to be learned from the events of 1914 is to be wary of analysts wielding historical analogies, particularly if they have a whiff of inevitability. War is never inevitable, though the belief that it is can become one of its causes."
– Joseph S. Nye, Jr.[1]

"Asia is more in a position of 19th-century Europe, where military conflict is not ruled out."
– Henry Kissinger at the 50th Munich Security Conference (MSC), January 31 to February 2, 2014[2]

Abstract:

This paper does not directly address current conflicts in Asia or assess the possibility of war between China and its neighboring countries over territorial and maritime disputes, but it does consider the question of how conflicts might be managed in order to achieve a long, durable era of peace throughout the Asia-Pacific in the 21st century. One model for managing conflict and competition in Asia is a "Concert of Powers," a systematically cooperative arrangement between regional great powers, exemplified by European diplomacy powers throughout the 19th and early 20th centuries. As China transforms itself and its role in the world, it may well position itself as a leading player in a concert of powers. China's offer to forge a new type of relationship with the US and other major powers can be viewed as an initial step in the formation of a concert of powers in the Asia-Pacific. The existing regional organizations and institutions in Asia can be seen as helpful adjuncts to any such arrangement, especially the ASEAN- and SCO-led network of regional security summits. Finally, this paper argues that if a modernized

---

[1] Joseph S. Nye, "1914 Revisited,"
<http://www.project-syndicate.org/commentary/joseph-s--nye-asks-whether-war-between-china-and-the-us-is-as-inevitable-as-many-believe-world-war-i-to-have-been>

[2] <http://www.bloomberg.com/news/2014-02-02/kissinger-says-asia-is-like-19th-century-europe-on-use-of-force.html>

concert of powers may be an approach to manage conflicts in Asia, Europe can assist the Asian powers by pioneering a modernized version of such a concert of powers. This would be a new way to develop European-Asian ties in the era of global security governance.

Key words: Chinese foreign policy, Concert of Powers, Chinese-US ties, the network of regional security organizations/institutions

Introduction

Leading Australian strategic thinkers, most notably Hugh White, have in recent years advanced the idea of a concert of powers as a possible solution to the region's security problems. In the context of intensifying competition, he argues, Beijing, Tokyo, and Washington might be induced into a concert of powers, similar to the Concert of Europe in the 19th century, to mitigate the most serious risks arising from Asia's changing distribution of power.[3] While all three would have to make very serious concessions, the choices are, in White's view, most stark for the US:[4] "As China's economy grows to become the world's largest, America has three choices: it can compete, share power or concede leadership in Asia. The choice is momentous – as significant for America's future as any it has faced."[5] This choice might be even more challenging than the competition during the Cold War because the economic foundations of China's rise portend a country with considerably more power than the Soviet Union could ever have hoped to attain. White argues that the best way for America to respond to China's growing power is to agree with China to share power and leadership in Asia. "This kind of order is hard to imagine, harder still to achieve, and if achieved, it would be difficult to maintain. It would hardly be worth considering if the alternatives were not so bad. But if there is any way to avoid both the dangers of Chinese domination and the risks of rivalry, it will be through a new order in which China's

---

[3] Sandy Gordon, "The quest for a concert of powers in Asia," Security Challenges, Vol. 8, No. 4 (Autumn 2012), 35.
[4] Jane Perlez, "Hugh White on 'The China Choice,'" October 2013, <http://sinosphere.blogs.nytimes.com/2013/10/16/hugh-white-on-the-china-choice/>.
[5] Hugh White, *The China Choice: Why America Should Share Power*, (Collingwood, Vic: Black Inc. 2012), back cover.

authority and influence grows enough to satisfy the Chinese, and America's role remains large enough to ensure that China's power is not misused."[6]

This article is not about the choice of the US and its allies in the region, but about China's choice with respect to the same problem.[7]

While China has not yet formally embraced the notion of a concert of powers, the discourse and practice of its foreign policy may, perhaps surprisingly, contain the seeds of enthusiasm for such an arrangement. Beijing, not Washington, could become a leading force in instantiating a concert of powers in Asia and the Pacific. Today, the continuation of America's uncontested hegemony in the region is uncertain, but for now and the foreseeable future, China can't replace the US and will be neither able nor willing to re-establish Chinese dominance. Nor are concepts like the G2 (a shared US-China hegemony, or China as a new de facto ally-class partner of the US-organized world order) or a new Cold War preferable models for solving Asia's security challenges. A new reality and promising trend in Asia and the Pacific is the peaceful coexistence of major powers including China, the US, Russia, India, and Japan with several middle and small powers. Therefore, a concert of powers goes beyond the above-mentioned concepts to Asian regional security.

This article outlines a new foreign policy for China, one which centers around a concert of powers adjusted for Asia's political and strategic circumstances. First, this paper argues that the transformation of Chinese foreign policy provides a historic opportunity to introduce a new model of regional security governance: a concert of powers. China's current and future foreign policy will be conducive to a concert of powers. Secondly, it examines China's new approach to dealing with the United States and conclude that a concert of powers in Asia may begin with the transformation of China-US relations —"a new type/model of great power relationship." Thirdly, it discusses the potential role of existing regional organizations/institutions in which China plays a key role. China already shaped the regional organizations from the ASEAN Security Community to the Shanghai Cooperation Organizations (SCO) in order to merge these institutions into regional "public goods," "public power," and "good governance" and into concerted Asian international

---

[6] Ibid., 129.

[7] This approach is based on my research and participation in the international project "A Twenty-First Century Concert of Powers," organized by the Peace Research Institute Frankfurt (PRIF),
<http://hsfk.de/A-Twenty-First-Century-Concert-of-Powers.763.0.html?&L=1>.

relations.[8] Finally, this paper outlines a possible role model for Europe in contributing to a 21st century concert of powers in Asia.

Part 1: Historic Transformation of Chinese Foreign Policy Increases the Necessity and Possibility of a Concert of Powers in Asia

Based on every indication, Chinese foreign policy is presently in transition, from its well-known "low-profile" approach (1989-2012) as a "peaceful rising power" to a pattern of behavior more closely resembling that of traditional great power diplomacy.[9] The transformation may even characterize the next decade (2013-2022), when China's current leadership will finish the second of its two five-year terms in office. The makers of Chinese foreign policy have always faced serious dilemmas. But now, contradictory imperatives in China's approach to the world have become more pronounced. Indeed, since 1989, Chinese foreign policy has been defined by a series of conflicting tendencies[10]:

- China's adherence to the principle of non-interference helps to consolidate relations with Southeast Asian nations (ASEAN) and India, even as China begins to adopt an approach to international security based on conditional intervention.[11] In short, China's foreign policy seeks to incorporate and strike a difficult balance between both the non-interference and intervention approaches.

- China has simultaneously become an existing international rules abider and a constructor of new rules in an increasingly Sino-centric regional order. In short, it helps to reform existing international rules and produces new international rules to govern a globalized world.

---

[8] The term "public power" comes from Jennifer Mitzen in the first chapter of *Power in Concert: the 19th Century Origins of Global Governance*, CUP, 2013.
[9] On the meaning of "keeping a low profile," see: Pang Zhongying, "Does China need a new foreign policy," presented at the SIPRI, Sweden, 16 April 2013, <http://books.sipri.org/files/misc/SIPRI-Hu%20Pang%20Zhongying.pdf>.
[10] Linda Jakobson, "China's foreign policy dilemma", 2013, <http://lowyinstitute.org/publications/chinas-foreign-policy-dilemma>.
[11] Pang Zhongying, "The Non-interference Dilemma: Adapting China's Approach to the New Context of African and International Realities," in IDSS (ed.), *China-Africa Relations: Governance, Peace and Security* (Ethiopia: 2013), 54-56.

- As the US declines relative to China and is commensurately less able or willing to provide Asian public goods to the extent that its Asian partners expect, China might not only fill the gap, but also replace the US as a dominant source of regional public goods both economically and strategically – albeit without fully supplanting American hegemony.

- China's political system, governance, and cultural orientation still differ considerably from Western-style democracy (most of China's Asian peers are democracies), but this does not mean that Chinese policy is completely antithetical or incompatible with that style of democracy. China's economic system is a free market system and therefore quite similar to that of the West's, although the Chinese government intervenes in the market to a greater extent. At the same time, China is intentionally cultivating more transparent governmental institutions, in accordance with dominant international norms of governance. The creation of an accountable counterpart for foreign nations in Beijing, for example the Chinese National Security Council, will help other nations communicate with the relevant institutions in China and assess who is in charge of making Chinese foreign policy.

- The importance of international cooperation dominates China's foreign policy. China has shifted its old attitudes to support multilateralism, regionally and globally. But at the same time, like its peer great powers, China has to secure itself and its interests in a competitive world, imposing limits on its capacity for cooperation.

- China's non-aligned position since the early 1980s is being called into question by the transformation of world politics. The benefits of China's non-aligned policy have been numerous, but China now has to seek partnerships with many countries to forge new types of potentially de facto alliance relationships. For example, a debate is currently underway on the possibility and necessity of a quasi-alliance between China and Russia. Furthermore, some advocate that China should resume its aligned policy; Yan Xuetong argues: "Through several recent speeches, Xi has articulated a different strategic direction. China's new foreign policy outlook indicates an approach known as *Fen Fa You Wei* (striving for achievement) to engage its neighboring countries and to over time align their interests with China's rise." He notes that Xi specifically stressed partnership between China and its neighbors. This shift seems to be more significant than it sounds. Under

Xi, China will begin to treat friends and enemies differently. For those who are willing to play a constructive role in China's rise, China will seek ways for them to gain greater actual benefits from China's development. "By tying up certain nations' incentives along with China's development, China will seek to build communities of common destinies with some of its key neighbors. We should expect these initiatives to cover [a] much wider range of strategic elements beyond mere economic interests." Eventually, this may even extend to providing security guarantees to selected countries. In the future, Yan Xuetong asserts: "China will decisively favor those who side with it with economic benefits and even security protections. On the contrary, those who are hostile to China will face much more sustained policies of sanctions and isolation."[12]

- China continues to seek peaceful resolution to its disputes with others, but also reserves the right to use force in defense of its sovereignty and territorial integrity. China is now negotiating a code of conduct (COC) with some Southeast Asian nations to solve territorial disputes in the South China Sea, and it repeatedly signals a desire to discuss its territorial dispute with Japan. China's military has improved greatly since 1979, when China engaged in its last foreign war with Vietnam. Since then, China has enjoyed at least three decades of peace.

- As a "rising power" in a newly multi-polar world, China views itself both as a "status quo power" and a "revisionist power." China wants to maintain the existing international order rather than overthrow it, but there is a widespread Chinese perception that the US alliances in the region, particularly the US-Japanese alliance, are designed as a containment mechanism to thwart China's "peaceful rise."[13] In Asia, some middle and small powers seem to continue challenging China's "core" interests, including China's territorial integrity. These challenges are urging China to revise its foreign policy into a more muscular approach. As a revisionist power, China is, of course, not satisfied with the existing hegemonic regional order. The declaration of China's Air Defense Identification Zone (ADIZ) exemplifies the point. In the past,

---

[12] Yan Xuetong, "China's new foreign policy: Not conflict but convergence of interests," <http://www.huffingtonpost.com/yan-xuetong/chinas-new-foreign-policy_b_4679425.html>.

[13] Wu Junfei, "An Analysis on the trilateral interactions among China, the US and Russia," Beijing: *Global Times*, April 24, 2013.

China had little choice but to tolerate the US-Japanese alliance and violations of Chinese sovereignty and rights. But today's China is no longer in the weak position of having to tolerate such affronts. At the 50th MSC, Chinese Ambassador Fu Ying, the Chair of the Foreign Affairs Committee of Chinese National People's Congress (NPS), highlighted the dilemma of regional inequality: "Do you know how long Japan already has such a defense zone? For 43 years. And how close it is to our territory? 130 km. So why don't you think China has any rights to set up the zone after more than 40 years? Why do we then risk the stability of the region? If Japan can do it, the United States and dozens of other countries, then why not China with a population of 1.3 billion and such a long coastline?"[14]

Here, a key question is: what does the transformation of Chinese foreign policy imply for conflict management in Asia?

In short, the transformation of Chinese foreign policy from a mess of contradictions into a cohesive strategy is a conducive force to build a concert of powers in/for Asia. A "21st Century Concert of Powers," as discussed by a research team organized by the Peace Research Institute Frankfurt, is an order in which "great powers ought to be peace-managers, bearing responsibility for peace, stability, and security of the whole system." In this approach, managing the peace "is not equal to preserving the status quo at all costs", but rather to "managing change smoothly when upholding peace so requires".[15]

If we compare the proposed 21st century concert of powers with the doctrines practiced by Chinese foreign policy in the past 25 years (from 1989 to the present), a chance of China adjusting the European concert of powers to the modern world can be seen to exist because China's evolving foreign policy is compatible with its basic premises. The notion of a concert of powers is not well understood and has not been widely embraced as a mechanism for preserving peace by scholars or practitioners of international politics.

---

[14] Quoted from "Wenn China provoziert wird, muss es hart reagieren," <http://www.focus.de/politik/ausland/chinas-wichtigste-aussenpolitikerin-china-wird-immer-als-bedrohung-dargestellt_id_3586960.html>.

[15] The 21st Century Concert Study Group, "A 21st Century Concert of Powers: Promoting Great Powers Multilateralism for the Post-Transatlantic Era," (Frankfurt: Peace Research Institute Frankfurt (PRIF), 2014), 74.

Part II: China's "New Model of Great Power Relations" with the US[16] – A First Step towards a Concert of Powers in Asia?

China's Offer and Its Dilemma

The management of relations with the US has been the "priority of priorities" in Chinese foreign policy since at least the early 1990s. Today, China's relationship with the US is at a historic crossroads. With the new political leadership in Beijing, China's approach to dealing with the US is changing. At least since the end of the 18th national congress of the Chinese Communist Party (CCP) in November 2012, China's new doctrine, "a new type of relationship between great countries" *(Xin Xing Da Guo Guan Xi)*, was promulgated to deal with the US.[17] Officially, China has disagreed with a persistent claim that a leading rising power like China will inevitably clash with the status quo power, in this case the self-declared "sole super power," the United States. China does, however, worry that such widespread perceptions may become a self-fulfilling prophecy, particularly if each side views the other through a competitive lens. That's why China should do everything possible to mitigate a sense of inevitability.

Since the mid-1970s, China has sought a stable and sustainable relationship with the US. But since 2008-2009, when the Obama administration was elected and the financial crisis along with the wars in Afghanistan and Iraq heightened perceptions of the "decline of the US", strategic distrust in Chinese-US relations has become steadily more pronounced.[18] In the context of America's economic problems, China's rise has increasingly come

---

[16] The term was originally translated as "a new type of relations between great countries" by the Chinese foreign ministry's professional translators, but, as a response, in the early 2013, the Obama administration understood it as "a new model of great power-based relations" with China. Now, Beijing adopts the "new model" but continues to use "major country relations" instead of "great power relations." See: Foreign Minister Wang Yi's speech "towards a new model of major-country relations between China and the United States," Washington: Brookings Institution, September 20, 2013.

[17] On the background and origins of the "new type of relations between great nations," see Zhang, Tuosheng's comment at <http://nautilus.org/napsnet/napsnet-special-reports/how-to-construct-a-new-u-s-china-great-power-relationship/#axzz2ZuEM9POO>.

[18] Wang Jisi and Kenneth G. Lieberthal, "Addressing U.S.-China Strategic Distrust," (Washington: Brookings Institution, March 30, 2012).

to be viewed as a major challenge to US primacy in the Asia-Pacific. This has led some scholars to begin re-conceptualizing the future of US-Chinese relations. Some advocate the formation of the Group of the Two (G2) with China, [19] a relationship between the existing superpower and the next superpower. President Obama visited Beijing in 2009. China's then-President Hu Jintao met his US counterpart frequently at various G20 summits and similar occasions, such as APEC meetings, to cooperatively manage the financial crisis and other global challenges. Unfortunately, though, a G2 model of US-Chinese relations was unlikely to eventuate in the way some US scholars anticipated or advocated.[20] Certain developments undermined the potential for such a new relationship. The Obama administration was frustrated by China's reluctance to fully cooperate with its ambitious domestic politics-driven agenda on climate change at the UN-orchestrated multilateral negotiations (UNFCCC) in Copenhagen. As a consequence of this, and of concerns by others about the possibility of joint US-Chinese hegemony, Chinese leaders abandoned the notion of a G2 without ever having embraced it.[21]

In the decades since the early 1990s, China has tended to be in a reactive position relative to the US, and relations between the two have historically been driven and shaped by the US. In many cases, China acquiesced to US preferences, despite periodic disagreements and reservations. However, in the context of the current US "pivot to Asia," China proactively offered a new kind of relationship: On December 6, 2011, in advance of a visit to the US by China's then-Vice President Xi Jinping, then-State Councilor Dai Bingguo issued a special article entitled "Adhere to the Path of Peaceful Development" to reassure the US that China would never challenge Washington's international leadership or deliberately seek to undermine the existing international order.[22] In February 2012, Xi prominently called for "a new type of relationship between China and the US, as two big nations in the world" to communicate his new policy to the US administration. At the 18th National Congress of the Chinese Communist Party in 2012, the phrase "a new type of international relations" was approved. At the NPC in March 2013, China's

---

[19] Zbigniew Kazimierz Brzezinski, "The Group of Two that could change the world," London: Financial Times, January 13, 2009.
[20] <http://www.foreignaffairs.com/articles/64946/elizabeth-c-economy-and-adam-segal/the-g-2-mirage>.
[21] In 2009 and after, Chinese then-leaders, particularly Premier Wen Jiabao, used several very important summits to say that China disagrees with the G2.
[22] <http://www.gov.cn/ldhd/2010-12/06/content_1760381.htm>.

new foreign policy, which formally included the pursuit of "a new type of relations with other great nations," was legislated.

President Xi explained to President Obama that "China and the United States must find a new path – one that is different from the inevitable confrontation and conflict between the major countries of the past. And that is to say the two sides must work together to build a new model of major country relationship based on mutual respect and win-win cooperation for the benefit of the Chinese and American peoples and people elsewhere in the world."[23] This "new type of relations between great nations" is seemingly a new manifestation of the G2, though with some important qualifications. By advocating the need for a "new type of relations," Beijing presses the US not only to recognize China's new status in the Asia-Pacific region, but also to register its opposition to the US "pivot to Asia," which Beijing views as a policy designed to contain China. President Xi remarked: "The vast Pacific Ocean has enough space for the two large countries of China and the United States."[24] This reflects China's concern that the US pivot does not leave enough space for a maritime China to fulfil its security rights and interests and instead tries to maintain the old US-dominated status quo in the Pacific.

One dilemma may be that a "new model of great power relations" might help to reduce conflicts, but without generating the level of respect and equality for China that its foreign policy is intended to attain. The US still finds it hard to acknowledge China's great power status and legitimate interests in the Asia-Pacific. If the US continues to subordinate a "new model of great power relations" with China to its alliance systems, the result could be enduring competition. China wants to have "win-win cooperation."

---

[23] Xi and Obama met the press after their summit, <http://www.whitehouse.gov/the-press-office/2013/06/08/remarks-president-obama-and-president-xi-jinping-peoples-republic-china->. "Xi calls for 'new' type of relations," <http://www.chinadaily.com.cn/china/2013-05/28/content_16537986.htm>.

[24] President Xi's before summit speech in California, June 7, 2013, <http://www.whitehouse.gov/the-press-office/2013/06/07/remarks-president-obama-and-president-xi-jinping-peoples-republic-china->.

America's Response and Its Dilemma

Many commentators in the US have faced the Chinese offer with ambivalence[25] because the dominant American perception is to refuse to accept that US power has really declined relative to China's. But today we live in a different world, and the US finds itself in the position of still being the most powerful state in the world but no longer in a super-power/absolute hegemonic status. Contradictorily, Samuel Huntington's *uni-multipolar* (differently from the "unipolar") moment may still be meaningful.[26]

The Obama administration has responded to the Chinese offer in a sophisticated and complex manner. For example, the former National Security adviser to the US President, Tom Donilon, judged the Chinese offer as "a new model for cooperation." He continued to say that "building a stable, productive, and constructive relationship with China" is one of the US's three strategic "pillars" in Asia-Pacific. He argued that "the United States welcomes the rise of a peaceful, prosperous China. We do not want our relationship to become defined by rivalry and confrontation. And I disagree with the premise put forward by some historians and theorists that a rising power and an established power are somehow destined for conflict." He emphasizes that there is nothing preordained about such an outcome. Power relations are not a law of physics, but a series of choices by leaders that lead to great power confrontation or cooperation. "Others have called for containment. We reject that, too. A better outcome is possible. But it falls to both sides—the United States and China—to build a new model of relations between an existing power and an emerging one. Xi Jinping and President Obama have both endorsed this goal."[27]

In June 2013, the Xi-Obama informal summit in California happened for the first time. It was assessed as a breakthrough[28] and a crucial step towards "a new type relations."[29] Allison Graham of Harvard University has argued that

---

[25] For example, just after the Xi-Obama summit in California, the Pacific Forum CSIS of the US published a comment authored by Brad Glosserman titled "A 'new type of great power relations'? Hardly," on PacNet, Number 40, June 10, 2013.

[26] Samuel Huntington, "The Lonely Superpower," Foreign Affairs, March/April 1999, 35-49.

[27] <http://www.whitehouse.gov/the-press-office/2013/03/11/remarks-tom-donilon-national-security-advisory-president-united-states-a>

[28] "Yang Jiechi on President Xi's summit with President Obama," Beijing: People's Daily, June 10, 2013

[29] Chinese Ambassador Cui Tiankai, Speech at the CSIS, Washington DC, May 25, 2013.

"[h]istory will judge this meeting not in terms of resolution of specific issues but rather on whether the leaders begin a serious conversation about building a new type of relationship between the two superpowers that bridges their rivalries and allows them to escape Thucydides'[s] Trap."[30] And US National Security Advisor Susan Rice reconfirmed that the US began to explore the concept and the substance of such a relationship with China: "When it comes to China, we seek to operationalize a new model of major power relations." That would mean managing inevitable competition while forging deeper cooperation on issues where our interests converge—in Asia and beyond. Both would seek the denuclearization of the Korean Peninsula, a peaceful resolution to the Iranian nuclear issue, a stable and secure Afghanistan, and an end to conflict in Sudan. She concluded by saying that there are opportunities for the US and China to take concerted action to bolster peace and development in places like sub-Saharan Africa, where sustainable growth would deliver lasting benefit to the peoples of Africa as well as to both countries.[31]

But by entering into a "new model of great power relations" with China, the US faces a dilemma: How to reorganize its relations with the existing alliance powers, especially regional countries like Japan, which has still not accepted a rising China, without arousing acute fears of abandonment. It is unclear what "a new model of great power relationship" with China means for the US alliance system in Asia. Japan feels considerable anxiety because its own interests might be subsumed by cooperation between China and the US. Indeed, China openly calls for co-managing Japanese revisionism with Washington under the auspices of a "new model of great power relations."[32] All of this will require major adaptations to America's longstanding alliance system, which is presently incompatible with the kind of systematically cooperative relationship with China that would need to operate at the heart of a concert of Asia. If this dilemma can be overcome, however, it may herald the emergence of a concerted trilateral relationship among the three major powers: China, Japan, and the US.

---

[30] Allison, Graham T. "Obama and Xi Must Think Broadly to Avoid a Classic Trap," New York Times, June 6, 2013.

[31] Susan Rice, "America's Future in Asia," speech at Georgetown University, November 20, 2013, <http://www.whitehouse.gov/the-press-office/2013/11/21/remarks-prepared-delivery-national-security-advisor-susan-e-rice>.

[32] The co-management of China and the US on Japan is a current argument in China and the Asia-Pacific.

Part III: How Regional Organizations in Asia Contribute to a Concert of Powers

According to Alexander Nikitin and Oleg Demidov, regional organizations can be defined as a "concert of concerts" of powers.[33] China has joined almost all regional organizations in the greater Asia-Pacific region. Not only is this remarkable, but China also began to take the lead in organizing the regional organizations.[34] An early Chinese casual leadership in the emergence of a new type of regional organizations is the Shanghai Cooperation Organization (SCO). China has hosted the SCO secretariat in Beijing from its beginning. Later on, from 2003-2009, China organized an ad hoc multilateral meeting called the "Six Party Talks" (China, North and South Korea, Japan, Russia, and the US) on the DPR Korea nuclear weapons issue. Additionally, China hosts the ASEAN-China Centre and other regional organizations.

The issue of the US presence as a non-Asian power with respect to geography in regional organizations in Asia is always contested and of the upmost importance. There are two kinds of regional organizations in the Asia-Pacific. One is composed of regional organizations with the US, and the other is without the US. The first kind includes APEC, ASEAN Regional Forum, Six Party Talks, and the Trans-Pacific Partnership (TPP), as well as the proposed but aborted organization the Asia-Pacific Community (APC), initially proposed by Australian Prime Minister Kevin Rudd. The second includes the SCO, ASEAN, the Chiang Mai Initiative (CMI), and the planned Regional Comprehensive Economic Partnership (RCEP), which is still being developed and negotiated. Unlike the US, China has fostered both kinds of regional organizations.

Some regional organizations are primarily economically and financially orientated but have an additional purpose of facilitating regional security coordination and cooperation. If we see these regional organizations as the basis of a concert of powers in Asia, the membership issue, a key issue in a

---

[33] Alexander Nikitin and Oleg Demidov, "Concert of concerts: Role of regional organizations in inter-state organizations in international system," in Harald Müller and Carsten Rauch (eds.), Academic Volume of the 21st Century Concert of Powers, PRIF project, forthcoming.

[34] See: Jia Qingguo, "The Shanghai Cooperation Organization: China's Experiment in Multilateral Leadership," 2007 Slavic Research Center (SRC), <http://www.isn.ethz.ch/Digital-Library/Publications/Detail/?ots591=0c54e3b3-1e9c-be1e-2c24-a6a8c7060233&lng=en&id=34993>.

possible 21st century concert of powers, can been solved successfully. Big powers, middle powers, and small powers each belong to these regional organizations. Fortunately and apparently, there does not exist the problem of exclusion and inclusion of small and great powers like in the G5/ G20.[35] A concert of powers can be seen as a kind of institution that provides regional public goods. Indeed, China has begun attempting to reshape its role to provide regional public goods. Before the 2010s, China confined itself to providing economic regional public goods. But in recent years, this has begun to change. There is an ongoing Chinese and international debate, for example, on China's provision of "a reliable nuclear umbrella" to some nations. This might even be a way to resolve the DPRK nuclear issue.[36]

Some Facts: China's Regional Policy for Asia[37]

1. There was no clear Chinese regional "Asia Policy" before 1997, when the Asian financial crisis happened.

2. After 1997, China gradually realized that it needs an Asia Policy. Based on China's conception of Asia, China is becoming the driving force for promoting East Asian economic cooperation. Ideas such as an "East Asian Community" emerged in China's Asia policymaking.

3. China has been a founding member of the Asia-Pacific Economic Cooperation (APEC) since 1989. The informal summit of the APEC was hosted after the "911" event in 2011 in Shanghai. China hosted the 2014 APEC summit in Beijing.

4. During the decade of General Secretary Hu Jintao (2002-2012), China elaborated its regional policy as "good neighbors" and "good partners" with

---

[35] PRIF, "The 21st Century Concert of Powers," Frankfurt 2015.
[36] Adam Cathcart, "Cooling the Nuclear Hotspot: Advocating a PRC Nuclear Umbrella for North Korea," <http://sinonk.com/2013/01/16/cooling-the-nuclear-hotspot-advocating-a-prc-nuclear-umbrella-for-north-korea/>.
[37] Pang Zhongying (2013), "Forging an Asian community: prospects and dilemmas," <http://www.foresightproject.net/downloads/FORESIGHT_CHINA_2013_PAGES_v14_WEB.pdf>, and Pang, Zhongying (2011), "Rebalancing Relations between East Asian and trans-Pacific Institutions: Evolving Regional Architectural Features", in *APEC and the Rise of China*, <http://www.thinkinchina.asia/wp-content/uploads/2_APEC_and_regional_architecture.pdf>.

all Asian countries based on the Chinese version of Asian/East Asian regionalism in economic and security cooperation.

5. China has been a strategic dialogue partner in the ASEAN Regional Forum (ARF) since 1996. ARF invites the US and other big powers to conduct annual multilateral dialogues.

6. In 2003, China was the first non-ASEAN member of the regional organization ASEAN to sign its Treaty of Amity and Cooperation in Southeast Asia (TAC) to rule out the possibility of using force to solve territorial disputes with some ASEAN nations.

7. In the post-Asian Financial Crisis years since 1997, China has been playing a leading role in East Asian monetary cooperation (the Chiang Mai Initiative mentioned above).

8. China and ASEAN nations have enjoyed a free trade agreement (FTA) since 2002.

9. China agreed to the Declaration on the Conduct of Parties in the South China Sea (DOC) and at the same time agreed to discuss a "Regional Code of Conduct in the South China Sea" (COC).

10. From 2003-2009, China mediated and chaired the Six Party Talks on the DPR Korea nuclear issue.

11. China shares co-leadership with Russia and Central Asian nations in organizing the Shanghai Cooperation Organization (SCO).

12. China becomes an observer member of the South Asian Association for Regional Cooperation (SAARC), while India and Pakistan become observer members of the SCO.

13. China-sponsored new international financial institution, with 31 members, including several key EU states, the Asian Infrastructure Investment Bank (AIIB) established formally in 2015.

Unlike in Europe, where institutions tend to be unified, cohesive, and largely distinct in function, there is remarkable overlap in the membership and functionality of Asia's regional organizations. If regional organizations signify to some degree a regional concert of powers, the overlapping of regional organizations are an indication of overlapped regional concert of powers. Hence, how to concert the concert of powers?

Some regional organizations such as the SCO are located in areas such as Central Asia, which are devoid of strong regional leadership.[38] Without a single hegemonic power, many big powers coexist and even cooperate. As China is an important political member in all Asian regional organizations, it can be indispensable in bridging various regional organizations in Asia in the direction of a concert of powers – or at least a concert of the regional organizations.

Finally, trilateral great power relations (for example between Japan, the US, and China) within the context of Asian regional groupings have the potential to foster the emergence of a concert of powers as a conflict management model. At present, there is a shortage of truly trilateral cooperation among big powers in the Asia-Pacific, but a truly trilateral great power relationship may now be emerging between China, India, and Russia. For example, China has been coordinating its Afghanistan policy with Russia and India.[39] If Chinese-Indian-Russian trilateral cooperation can be sustained, it would be a core or basis of a regional concert of powers in Asia. In stark contrast to the situation before World War I, such a concert of powers should not merge into a binary alliance system, but should consist of different great powers in Asia plus the US, which are all part of different and overlapping Asian organizations.

Concluding Remarks: Building a Concert of Powers Based on the "New Coexistence" Policy of Powers

How can China contribute to the formation of a concert of powers in Asia? Firstly, by combining its "peaceful rise" and newly initiated "great power diplomacy" doctrines in its foreign policy. Zheng Bijian, who is a leading politician to use the concept of "China's peaceful rise" coined by scholars including the author of this paper, clearly denies any analogy between today's China and Japan/Germany before World War I or the Soviet Union. He considers that the latter's rise to world power status led to total wars: "China

---

[38] The term "no one's lands" comes from a conference title "Security in a no one's world: Game changers," The NATO Defense College Foundation, Rome, February 13-14, 2014.

[39] Ankit Panda, "Is Trilateral China-India-Russia Cooperation in Afghanistan Possible?" The Diplomat, January 16, 2014, <http://thediplomat.com/2014/01/is-trilateral-china-india-russia-cooperation-in-afghanistan-possible/>

will not follow the path of Germany leading up to World War I or those of Germany and Japan leading up to World War II, when these countries violently plundered resources and pursued hegemony. Neither will China follow the path of the great powers vying for global domination during the Cold War. Instead, China will transcend ideological differences to strive for peace, development, and cooperation with all countries of the world."[40]

Firstly, China began its process of "peaceful rise" in the late 1970s. The 1992-2012 period is a key decade of China's "peaceful rise."[41] Today, as China faces so many huge challenges from its own transformation, it has no choice but to reform its foreign policy, but this change is still at an early stage. To achieve this goal, China has to modernize its foreign policy principles and institutions.

Secondly, building of a new model of great power relations with the US is a good starting point in building a concert of powers in the Asia-Pacific region, but it may not go far enough. At this point, Chinese decision makers and practitioners apply the "new model of great power relations" only to Chinese-US ties. This should be extended to all Asian nations. Hoang Anh Tuan from Vietnam writes: "China only offers to establish this 'new type of great power relationship' with the US, not with any other powers. The 'new type of relationship' was not intended to alter Beijing's ties with India, Russia, or Japan. This suggests that the Middle Kingdom views itself as an equal with the US, and sees the 'new type of great power relationship' as a step in the direction of building a 'mini order' that could be conveniently employed to resolve bilateral, regional, and global issues."[42] This observation may be right because even China's top diplomat says that this "new type of relations" specially aims to reframe its relations with the US.[43] However, China does not consider the US and itself the only great countries or great powers in today's world. Based on the well-known "multi-polar" world argument, China has made clear that it hopes to establish a new type of relations with all other powers. Since the early 1990s, when the US unilaterally declared the "uni-

---

[40] Zheng Bijian, "China's 'peaceful rise' to great power status," *Foreign Affairs*, September/October 2005.

[41] Pang Zhongying, "Does China need a new foreign policy?" a keynote presentation at a SIPRI conference "Chinese Foreign Policy under Hu Jintao," Stockholm, April 18-19, 2013.

[42] Hoang Anh Tuan, "Snowden saga exposes fragile US-China ties," Asia Times Online, <http://www.atimes.com/atimes/China/CHIN-03-170713.html>.

[43] Yang Jiechi, "Innovations in China's diplomatic theory and practice under new conditions," <http://www.fmprc.gov.cn/eng/zxxx/>.

polarity" of the post-Cold War world, China has envisioned a multi-polar world and has been playing a role in promoting and managing a trend towards multi-polarity or even hyper-polarity. A fundamental question: what is new in China's "new model of great power relations"? If the new model of great power relations means a concert of powers, it would definitely be new.

Thirdly, China should help recognize the regional complex coexistence of powers and use a concert of powers to manage that complexity. The US PACOM commander, Navy Adm. Samuel J. Locklear III, calls the Asia-Pacific "the most militarized region in the world," but he argues that "ultimately, for mutual security, China and its military must be regional leaders and coexist in its part of the world with US allies and with US and allied militaries," and that "they're going to have to work hard to get through some of the [...] territorial disputes they're having with their neighbors. We [the US] don't take sides on the territorial disputes," "but we do expect them to be done peacefully."[44] This is China's choice.

Nearly 60 years ago at the 1955 Bandung Conference (Afro-Asian Conference) in Indonesia, "New China" – the People's Republic of China (PRC) was just established – called for "peaceful coexistence" with other powers. But a positive, peaceful coexistence was never realized in Asia and the Pacific. Between China and the US, there has only been negative peaceful coexistence since 60 years ago. In the Asia-Pacific, coexistence is extremely complex: China coexists not only with the US but with the US-led regional alliance system, various Asian-Pacific regional institutions coexist, and China has to live with its friends and foes in the region. It is highly unlikely and undesirable that a concert of powers could or even should replace the existing regional structure of security arrangements, but we can introduce a concert of powers as a supplement to the existing Asia-Pacific regional security system as the old hegemonic, post-World War II and post-Cold War regional order in the Asia-Pacific continues to erode.

Fourthly, China can take the lead in building a concert of powers with Chinese peculiarities. This article considers the function of a concert of powers in Asia-Pacific as follows:

---

[44] Cheryl Pellerin, American Forces Press Service, <http://www.pacificnewscenter.com/index.php?option=com_content&view=article&id=41578:admiral-locklear-rebalance-to-asia-pacific-region-on-track&catid=45:guam-news&Itemid=156>

- It could provide a new option for the Asia-Pacific to reorganize international relations in a more peaceful direction.
- It could be an important platform and opportunity to transform the long "negative peace" between the US and its allies and China to a positive peace in the Asia-Pacific.
- It can offer an opportunity for middle and small powers to avoid having to take on the wrenching decision between the US or China.
- From a global security governance perspective,[45] the introduction of a concert of powers could better help regional security governance.

From the long term perspective, it is a necessary alternative to the end of Pax Americana in order to avoid regional disorder in the Asia-Pacific. A concert of powers is not designed for a hegemonic world, but for a post-hegemonic one. Although many Americans and non-Americans still refuse to think that the US is no longer the only superpower, we have to prepare for a post-hegemonic world in which the US as well as China will have to be a part.[46] China's choices will be decisive as to whether a concert of powers emerges in Asia, and if so, whether it can live up to expectations.

---

[45] Jennifer Mitzen, *Power in Concert: The 19th Century Origins of Global Governance* (Chicago: University of Chicago Press, 2013).

[46] Robert Keohane, *After Hegemony: Cooperation and Discord in the World Political Economy, 1st edition* (Princeton: Princeton University Press, 1984).

Dedication of World War I memorial in Shanghai, 1924

Revisiting the First Modern Arms Race Leading to World War I: Implications for the Asian Rebalance

Antulio J. Echevarria II

Abstract:

Historians and social scientists have long debated whether arms races cause wars, and the First World War has served as a classic case study.[1] The consensus view is Germany feared falling behind France and Russia in 1914, and chose to take the offensive rather than allow the situation to grow worse.[2] This particular arms race—the first facilitated by the full infrastructure and machinery of the Industrial Revolution and its late nineteenth-century byproduct, the Technological Revolution—actually began well before 1914. It also ended several decades after 1918, with Great Britain, Japan, and the United States competing for naval supremacy well into the Second World War. Before it was over, the first modern arms race produced an unprecedented quantity and quality of arms, added two new domains to modern warfare (underwater and air), and involved all the leading nations of Europe, North America, and Asia.[3]

---

[1] Compare: Toby J. Rider, Michael G. Findley, and Paul F. Diehl, "Just Part of the Game? Arms Races, Rivalry, and War," Journal of Peace Research 48, no. 1 (January 2011), 85-100; Craig Etcheson, *Arms Race Theory: Strategy and Structure of Behavior* (New York, 1989); Paul M. Kennedy (ed.), *The War Plans of the Great Powers, 1880-1914* (Boston, 1985); Teresa Clair Smith, "Arms Race Instability and War," Journal of Conflict Resolution 24 (June 1980), 253-84; A.J.P. Taylor, *How Wars Begin* (London, 1979); Lewis F. Richardson, *Arms and Insecurity* (Pacific Grove, CA, 1960); Samuel Huntington, "The Arms Race Phenomena," Public Policy (1958), 1-20.

[2] For the consensus view see: Annika Mombauer, *Helmuth von Moltke and the Origins of the First World War* (Cambridge and New York, 2001); Niall Fergusson, *Pity of War* (New York, 1999); David Stevenson, *Armaments and the Coming of the War: Europe, 1904-1914* (Oxford, 1996); David G. Herrmann, *The Arming of Europe and the Making of the First World War* (Princeton, 1996). Robert K. Massie, *Dreadnought: Britain, Germany and the Coming of the Great War* (New York, 1992); A.J.P. Taylor, *War by Time-Table: How the First World War Began* (London, 1969). Recent approaches prefer contingency over causality; representative is Christopher Clark, *The Sleepwalkers: How Europe Went to War in 1914* (New York, 2014).

[3] For more on the arms race, see: Antulio J. Echevarria II, "The Arms Race: Qualitative and Quantitative Aspects," in *War. Volume IV: War and the Modern World*, Roger Chickering, Dennis Showalter, and Hans van de Ven (eds.), (Cambridge, 2012), 163-80.

One can find any number of historical differences between today's world and that of a century ago, and only a few are needed to make drawing lessons from that period risky.[4] While learning from the experiences of others is rarely as easy or as useful as Bismarck so famously implied, we would do well to learn whatever we can from the costly decisions of 1914. However imperfect or subjective that knowledge might be, we can still benefit from it. Every form of knowledge has its limitations, and historical knowledge is no different. Nonetheless, reexamining the dynamics of the world's first modern arms race can still give rise to important, if particular, insights, some of which surely ought to inform contemporary strategy. This is especially true given the United States' aim of rebalancing its strategic focus toward Asia, and the potential for that reorientation to spark an arms race with the Peoples Republic of China (PRC).

To be clear, official US policies regarding the rebalance repeatedly underscore the importance of promoting peaceful and productive engagement. The 2011 US National Military Strategy, for instance, states that America "seeks a positive, cooperative, and comprehensive relationship with China" and desires to "expand areas of mutual interest and benefit, improve understanding, reduce misperception, and prevent miscalculation."[5] Moreover, Washington and Beijing have publically proclaimed their peaceful intentions, and their respective defense secretaries have announced plans for building stronger military-to-military contacts to facilitate the strategic dialogue that has been in place more or less since the Nixon administration.[6] Former US Secretary of State Hilary Clinton has gone so far as to reject any comparisons to the Cold War model or to the West's former strategy of containment:

> The United States is attempting to work with a rising power to foster its rise as an active contributor to global security, stability, and prosperity while also sustaining and securing American leadership in a changing world. And we are trying to do this without entering into *unhealthy competition, rivalry, or conflict*; [...] We are, together, building a model in which we strike a stable and mutually acceptable *balance between cooperation and competition*. This is uncharted territory. And we have to get it right, because so much depends on it. [...] So to those who ask, "Is the United States

---

[4] For greater detail on the pitfalls of using history, see: Antulio J. Echevarria II, "The Trouble with History," Parameters 35, no. 2 (Summer 2005), 78-90.

[5] Admiral Michael Mullen, The National Military Strategy of the United States 2011 (Washington, DC: Dept. of Defense, 2011), 14.

[6] Dong Wang, "The Xi-Obama Moment: A Post-Summit Assessment," National Bureau of Asian Research, October 21, 2013,
<http://www.nbr.org/research/activity.aspx?id=367>.

attempting to *contain* China?" Our answer is a clear no. In fact, the United States helped pave the way for China to be where it is today in its own development.[7]

Nonetheless, the potential for *"unhealthy competition, rivalry, or conflict"* is present, even if the intention is not. Settling the territorial disputes in the South China Sea and the East China Sea will pose challenges to the *"balance between cooperation and competition,"* particularly as the demand for oil and other resources increases with the growth of Pacific Rim economies. Consequently, both sides may feel pressure on occasion to reassert their claims, pressure that some experts have already applied.[8] Such reassertions, should they involve military forces, will amount to a de facto arms race. Thus far, recent clashes over the disputed territories (as between China and Vietnam in 1974 and 1988) have fortunately not escalated into a general war between China and the United States; however, containing them will only grow more difficult over time as political and economic stakes increase. According to some experts, moreover, an arms buildup, if not a race per se, is already underway.[9] China recently established an air defense identification zone (ADIZ) overlapping those of Japan and South Korea, deployed its first aircraft carrier (with four or more under construction), expanded its fleet of nuclear ballistic missile and attack submarines, built a new submarine base in the South China Sea, increased its investment in aerial refueling, and put in service two new destroyers (Type 052D).[10] Beijing's official defense

---

[7] Secretary of State Hillary Rodham Clinton, U.S. Institute of Peace China Conference, March 7, 2012,
<http://iipdigital.usembassy.gov/st/english/texttrans/2012/03/201203081765.html#axzz32kc1mzQa>. Emphasis added.

[8] Andrew S. Erickson, "China's Near-Seas Challenges," The National Interest 129 (January/February 2014): 60-66; Leszek Buszynski, "The South China Sea: Oil, Maritime Claims, and US-China Strategic Rivalry," Washington Quarterly 33, no. 2 (Spring 2012), 139-56.

[9] Evan Braden Montgomery, "Contested Primacy in the Western Pacific: China's Rise and the Future of US Power Projection," International Security 38, no. 4 (Spring 2014), 115-49.

[10] Jacqueline Newmyer Deal, "Red Alert," The National Interest 131 (May/June 2014), 86-87. For a broader survey of China's defense capabilities, see: David Shambaugh, *China Goes Global: The Partial Power* (Oxford: Oxford University, 2013), 269-306.

expenditures for 2013 show a 10.7 percent increase over 2012, a rate commensurate with the reported growth of China's economy.[11]

Furthermore, despite official pronouncements, some Chinese authorities and defense experts are dismissive of Washington's assurances, believing instead the United States is "following a policy of containment, thinly disguised in the Obama administration's 're-balance.'"[12] Indeed, deep and perhaps irreconcilable differences exist between the United States and China over human rights, military modernization, and how to pursue regional security along the Pacific Rim. Those differences and others do not necessarily mean an armed clash is inevitable, but the potential for coercive practices by both parties remains high. Whether the PRC is really the power it represents itself as being, which some question, may not matter.[13] Perceptions may be the real determining factors, and self-perceptions most of all. Certainly that was the case a century ago.

Part I

The first modern arms race warrants re-examination *not* because arms races cause major wars—they do not, as the armaments programs of the Cold War demonstrated. Rather, the first arms race of the twentieth century is instructive because it reflected, and was in fact produced by, a larger competition among major powers for greater political influence, as is the case along the Pacific Rim. All the major powers, but especially Britain and Germany, used the arms race—or its individual armaments programs—as a political tool, either to deter or coerce their rivals, and thereby to enhance their own political influence. Indeed, the military strategy of deterrence and its inverse, coercion, underpinned the first arms race of the twentieth century, and served to link it to the larger political aim of increased influence, even dominance.

---

[11] International Institute for Strategic Studies, *The Military Balance 2014*, James Hackett (ed.), (London: Routledge, February 2014), 209-10; the percentage is not believed to be reflective of the PRC's true defense outlays.

[12] Nina Hachigian (ed.), *Debating China: The US-China Relationship in Ten Conversations* (Oxford: Oxford University, 2014), 223.

[13] David Shambaugh, "The Illusion of Chinese Power," The National Interest 132 (July/August 2014), 39-48.

For the purposes of this article, deterrence simply means making people decide *not* to do something, such as launch an invasion, whereas coercion means compelling them to *do* a specific thing, such as granting concessions or complying with the terms of a treaty.[14] A military strategy of deterrence means having enough armed might on hand to make an adversary believe an act of aggression will either be defeated or cost more than it is worth. Strategies of deterrence are commonly thought of in four ways: direct, or discouraging an attack on oneself; extended, or dissuading an attack on a friend or ally; general, or deterring a potential threat; and immediate, or dissuading an imminent attack.[15] Military strategies of coercion generally make use of intimidation (or coercive or armed diplomacy), punishment, or denial.[16] Intimidation or coercive diplomacy was the most important form for the era before the First World War; it is simply the practice of using military power—as in mobilizing one's forces, conducting training exercises along a border, or initiating an armaments program—to threaten an adversary into complying with one's demands. The key, of course, is that the threat of force can be controlled.

An arms race is defined here as a competition among rivals to surpass (or keep pace with) each other militarily. Arms races typically involve several armaments programs, and can take on both quantitative and qualitative dimensions. They often produce accidental asymmetries or imbalances in military capabilities due in part to the nonlinear nature of technological change and to such factors as economic and geographic resources and strategic alliances. Britain, France, Russia, and Germany, for instance, competed aggressively in the first modern arms race; but Britain placed more emphasis on sustaining her naval supremacy, while the others ultimately gave higher priorities to land power. Air power was an entirely new domain, and while pundits such as H.G. Wells (*The Air War*, 1908) speculated as to whether it might become a game-changer, it was not technologically mature enough by 1914 to upset the balance of power.

---

[14] See: Daniel Byman and Matthew Waxman, *The Dynamics of Coercion: American Foreign Policy and the Limits of Military Might* (Cambridge: Cambridge University, 2002).

[15] Paul K. Huth, *Extended Deterrence and the Prevention of War* (Yale: Yale University, 1991).

[16] Some define coercive diplomacy as a form of mediation or negotiation, and thus as an alternative to armed conflict rather than a type of military strategy. Alexander L. George, *Forceful Persuasion: Coercive Diplomacy as an Alternative to War* (Washington, DC: US Institute of Peace, 1997).

Part II

The first modern arms race essentially started with Great Britain's naval bill of 1889; the bill formally announced the "two-power standard," which meant the Royal Navy would maintain a fighting power "at least equal to the strength of any two other countries."[17] At the time, the Royal Navy was already as strong as the next two largest navies, the French and Russian. However, the bill called for an additional 10 battleships, 42 cruisers, and 18 torpedo gunships to be built over the next five years.[18] It was clearly an attempt at general deterrence designed to guarantee British naval supremacy through the *fin de siècle*. Nevertheless, maintaining the two-power standard was an ambitious task; even a modest expansion by either France or Russia would force Britain to redouble her efforts, which in fact happened. Both France and Russia increased their naval armaments programs in the early 1890s in direct response to British expansion. Britain, in turn, responded by adding 3 more battleships to her original target of 10, and by implementing a new five-year plan designed to add 12 additional battleships and 20 cruisers by the end of the century.[19]

The Japanese, too, entered the naval arms race with a ten-year naval expansion program after demolishing the Chinese navy in the first Sino-Japanese War (1894-95).[20] By the end of that ten-year period, Japan had

---

[17] JonTesuro Sumida, *In Defense of Naval Supremacy: Finance, Technology, and British Naval policy 1889-1914* (Annapolis, 2014); Lawrence Sondhaus, *Naval Warfare, 1815-1914* (New York, 2001), 161; Roger Parkinson, *The Late Victorian Navy: The Pre-Dreadnought Era and the Origins of the First World War* (Suffolk, 2008).

[18] The bill also reversed the 1886 decision to suspend the building of battleships due to their increased vulnerability to underwater mines, submarines, torpedoes, and fast torpedo boats. By the late 1880s, capital ships were vulnerable to inexpensive mines and torpedoes. Germany, Austria-Hungary, Italy, Spain, and Japan considered embracing the approach of the jeune école, security fleets with small, highly maneuverable vessels. However, during the next decade improved propulsion for larger ships, rapid-firing cannon, better fire-control mechanisms for engaging smaller craft, and torpedo-boat destroyers offset the threats posed earlier, and shifted the balance back in favor of capital ships. Arne Roksund, *The Jeune École: The Strategy of the Weak* (Leiden, 2007).

[19] Paul M. Kennedy, *The Rise and Fall of British Naval Mastery* (London, 1991 [1976]).

[20] Japan's naval victory established it as Asia's preeminent power. US Secretary of the Navy, Hilary A. Herbert, remarked that "Japan had leaped, almost at one bound, to a place among the great nations of the earth." S. C. M. Paine, *The Sino-Japanese War of 1894-1895: Power, Perceptions, and Primacy* (Cambridge, 2003), 3; Benjamin A. Elman, "Naval Warfare and the Refraction of China's Self-Strengthening Reforms into

emerged victorious from the Russo-Japanese War (1904-05), and her navy, built mostly in Britain (listed 6 battleships, 17 cruisers, 24 destroyers, and over 60 torpedo boats), essentially gave her mastery of the seas in the Western Pacific, save for growing British and American influence there.[21] The Americans also began building a capital fleet in the early 1890s, though less to catch the Royal Navy than to protect their own maritime interests, which were growing rapidly. By the Spanish-American War (1898), the United States had increased its navy from a handful of obsolete craft to a modern fleet of 6 battleships, 2 armored cruisers, and several light cruisers.[22] America's influence in the Philippines and surrounding areas increased with her victory over the Spanish in 1898.

In 1906, *Jane's Fighting Ships*, a popular yet authoritative military science publication, ranked Britain first among major naval powers; the United States, France, Japan, Germany, Russia, Italy, and Austria-Hungary followed in order.[23] However, in the same year, the British commissioned the *HMS Dreadnought*, the first of a new class of battleship that rendered all previous designs obsolete, including some 50 capital ships already in service in the Royal Navy.[24] The *Dreadnought* was almost fifty percent larger, armed with twice as many guns, each with a range of more than twice that of earlier guns, and was ten to twenty percent faster. Four years later, the production of so-called "super dreadnoughts," which carried even larger guns, rendered dreadnought-class battleships obsolete. These super dreadnoughts were eclipsed just three years later by Queen Elizabeth class battleships, armed

---

Scientific and Technological Failure, 1865-1895," in *Naval History 1850-Present*, ed. Andrew Lambert (Aldershot and Burlington, 2007).

[21] David C. Evans and Mark R. Peattie, *Kaigun: Strategy, Tactics, and Technology in the Imperial Japanese Navy, 1887–1941* (Annapolis, MD, 1997); R.M. Connaughton, *The War of the Rising Sun and the Tumbling Bear—A Military History of the Russo-Japanese War 1904–5* (London, 1988); J.N. Westwood, *Russia against Japan, 1904-1905: A New Look at the Russo-Japanese War* (Albany, 1986).

[22] Al Nofi, *The Spanish-American War 1898* (Conshohocken, PA, 1996), 100-11.

[23] Fred T. Jane, *Jane's Fighting Ships* (New York, 1906-07).

[24] Nicholas Lambert, *Sir John Fisher's Naval Revolution* (Columbia, 2002). In 1905, a state-of-the-art battleship displaced 13,000 tons, and was armed with four 12-inch guns with a range of 6,000 yards. The HMS Dreadnought displaced 18,000 tons, was armed with ten 12-inch guns, and could reach speeds of 21 knots. Cruisers and destroyers also doubled in size, firepower, and speed: in 1905, they displaced 500 tons, and were armed with 3-inch guns and some small-diameter torpedoes; by 1914, they displaced nearly 1,000 tons, could reach speeds of 35 knots, and were armed with four 4-inch guns and several 21-inch torpedoes. D. K. Brown, *Warrior to Dreadnought: Warship Development 1860–1905* (Annapolis, MD, 2003).

with eight 15-inch guns.[25] The pace of technological change at sea was clearly accelerating, but the value of battleships would suffer from a nonlinear technological turn as the capabilities of aircraft carriers increased after the Great War.

In 1913, *Jane's Fighting Ships* still showed Britain ranked first among naval powers by a wide margin; however, Germany had moved into second, displacing the United States, which dropped to third; and France and Japan were tied for fourth.[26] Rather than merely deterring naval competition and securing mastery of the seas for the British Empire, the bill of 1889 set in motion a global naval arms race. It did so at a hefty albeit still affordable cost for Britain.[27]

Similar dynamics also played out in the land-power domain of the arms race. After the Second Moroccan Crisis, for instance, Germany passed two army bills (1912 and 1913).[28] The former added 29,000 men to the German army and authorized technological, organizational, and logistical improvements. However, it was deemed inadequate almost immediately, especially given the rapid rate of the Russian army's reforms and expansion after its losses in the Russo-Japanese War and the ensuing mutiny; hence, the enactment of the 1913 army bill, which added 137,000 more men to the army.[29] The bills were intended to redress the perceived imbalance of military power on land and to serve as a deterrent. However, the French responded by introducing a plan to reinstate three-year (instead of two-year) military service, which would keep more military personnel on active duty longer while new ones were conscripted and trained. The Russians, too, promised to increase the size of their army, though results were not expected until the summer of 1914.[30]

---

[25] Siegfried Breyer, *Battleships and Battlecruisers of the World, 1905–1970* (London, 1973). In 1910, dreadnought-class battleships were themselves rendered obsolete by the production of so-called "super dreadnoughts," typified by the HMS Orion, which carried ten 13.5-inch guns. These massive ships were in turn superseded in 1913 by yet another generation of battleships—the Queen Elizabeth class—which was armed with eight 15-inch guns. This class of warship continued to serve throughout World War II, although its value diminished as the power of aircraft carriers grew.

[26] Fred T. Jane, *Jane's Fighting Ships* (New York, 1912-13).

[27] British naval expenditures after 1889 doubled compared to the previous ten-year period. Kennedy, *Rise and Fall of British Naval Mastery*.

[28] Herrmann, *Arming of Europe*, 161-66. For a broader context see Hew Strachan, *The First World War. Vol. I: To Arms* (Oxford, 2004), 1-34.

[29] Gordon Craig, *Germany 1866-1945* (Oxford, 1978).

[30] In the winter of 1912-13, the Russian Defense Minister, Vladimir Sukholminov, told the French military attaché, General de Laguiche: "Germany is in a very critical position. It

Air power was obviously the youngest and probably the most anticipated domain of the arms race. By 1910 and 1911, French and German military aircraft were participating in maneuvers, though primarily in reconnaissance roles.[31] At the same time, military planners were considering ways in which aircraft, as yet an underdeveloped weapon, might be used to terrorize civilian populations through bombing raids.[32] Had the technology matured quickly enough, aircraft and the threat of bombing would likely have been used to coerce, as in the early stages of the Second World War. Nonetheless, the many displays of France's aerial prowess that took place between 1905 and 1914 were certainly designed to impress, if not intimidate. The 1913 edition of *Jane's All the World's Aircraft* reported the French in the lead with 421 military airplanes and 14 dirigibles on hand; the Germans ranked second with 200 airplanes (and 200 under construction) and 10 dirigibles; the British were in third place with 142 fixed-wing aircraft and 7 dirigibles.[33]

Part III

The naval arms race also afforded opportunities for the exercise of coercive diplomacy. One of the more infamous examples of such attempts was the so-called risk theory (*Risikogedanke*) introduced by Grand Admiral Alfred von Tirpitz, Secretary of State of the Imperial Naval Office in the years before the Great War. In brief, the theory aimed at building a fleet strong enough to pose an unacceptable risk to Britain, and thereby coerce London into a power-sharing relationship that (it was hoped) might include concessions in the form

---

is encircled by enemy forces: to the west France, to the east Russia—and it fears them." Herrmann, *Arming of Europe*, 191.

[31] Fred T. Jane, *Jane's All the World's Airships* (New York, 1909), published its first volume in 1909, but had few military aircraft to report. Lee Kennett, *The First Air War, 1914-1918* (New York, 1991).

[32] In 1913, the US Secretary of War reported on aeronautical appropriations by country: France led the way with expenditures of $7.4 million dollars, followed by Germany and Russia with $5 million each; England and Italy trailed with $3 million and $2.1 million respectively. I. B. Holley, Jr., *Ideas and Weapons* (Washington, DC., 1997), 29.

[33] Fred T. Jane, *Jane's All the World's Aircraft* (New York, 1913). Operational readiness varied almost daily. The figures did not reflect the number of civilian aircraft, or pilots active in the many national aviation societies and clubs across Europe and the United States. These societies provided a ready source of experienced pilots and supplemental aircraft in time of war.

of bases and access to markets.[34] Such a relationship would clearly enhance German prestige and influence, giving it a proverbial "place in the sun." The initial vehicle for achieving this was Germany's naval bill of 1898, which appropriated funds for a navy of 19 battleships, 42 cruisers, and sundry supporting vessels.[35] Two years later, a second naval bill was issued that set a seventeen-year deadline to construct a fleet of 2 flagships, 36 battleships, and 45 cruisers.[36]

However, Tirpitz's theory was based upon assumptions that failed to hold up in the fluid strategic environment of the *fin de siècle*. His first such assumption was that Germany's growing shipbuilding capacity could successfully challenge Britain's. This belief was not unreasonable since Britain was involved in the Second Boer War (1898-1902) and faced substantial cost outlays. Moreover, Germany's economic growth to this point had been phenomenal: between 1889 and 1913, her gross national product had doubled, while that of Britain had grown by only two-thirds.[37] By 1914, Germany was self-evidently the most powerful industrial nation in the world after the United States. However, it struggled to challenge Britain's vast shipbuilding complex. Even though Britain's Liberals, who took office in 1905, favored less defense spending, their agenda did not last, and overall expenditures remained sufficient. Second, he assumed Britain would not seek an alliance with another naval power, given its desire to maintain naval supremacy relative to the two-power standard. However, London, in fact, concluded an alliance with Japan in 1902, which would endure until 1921. It also engaged the Russians in a formal entente in 1907.

---

[34] Paul M. Kennedy, "Tirpitz, England, and the Second Navy Law of 1900: A Strategical Critique," Militärgeschichtliche Mitteilungen 8 (1970), 38; Mombauer, "German War Plans," 66.

[35] Annika Mombauer, "German War Plans," in *War Planning 1914*, Richard F. Hamilton and Holger Herwig (eds.), (Cambridge, 2010), 65-66; Michael Epkenhans, "Wilhelm II and 'His' Navy, 1888-1918," in *The Kaiser: New Research on Wilhelm II's Role in Imperial Germany*, Annika Mombauer and Wilhelm Deist (eds.), (Cambridge, 2003); and *Die Wilhelminische Flottenrüstung, 1908-1914. Weltmachtstreben, Industrieller Fortschritt, Soziale Integration* (Munich, 1991).

[36] Rolf Hobson, *Imperialism at Sea: Naval Strategic Thought, the Ideology of Sea Power, and the Tirpitz Plan, 1875-1914* (Boston, 2002).

[37] While steel production grew by 350 percent in Britain, it increased almost 1,500 percent in Germany (and by more than 8,600 percent in the United States); coal output rose by 650 percent in Germany, compared to 250 percent in Britain. S.B. Clough, *The Economic Development of Western Civilization* (New York, 1959), 377, 385; W.O. Henderson, *The Rise of German Industrial Power, 1834-1914* (Berkeley, 1975), 233-4; B.R. Mitchell, *European Historical Statistics 1750-1970* (London, 1975), 818-26.

These arrangements essentially allowed the Royal Navy to secure its flanks in the Mediterranean Sea and in the western Pacific and to reduce its vulnerability to the risk theory. Third, Tirpitz did not take into account the bleed-over of the arms race's other regimes, namely the land and air domains. Each of these required increased expenditures over time. In fact, the Reich's production of heavy battleships actually declined after 1912, as the focus of German armaments shifted to land power via the army bills of 1912 and 1913. German investments in fixed-wing aircraft also skyrocketed, increasing from 36,000 marks in 1909 to 26 million marks by 1914.[38] This amount was still small compared to the naval bill of 1898, which had approved 400 million marks for shipbuilding. Nonetheless, it was clear that time had simply run out for the Tirpitz plan.

The naval arms race between Britain and Germany ended informally in 1913, and with it the Reich's attempt to win a "place in the sun" through coercive diplomacy.[39] Germany had managed to put into service 46 capital ships (17 dreadnoughts, 21 pre-dreadnoughts, and 9 cruisers); however, Britain had built 103 capital ships (29 dreadnoughts, 40 pre-dreadnoughts, and 34 cruisers). Tirpitz's goal had been a ratio of 2:3 German to British capital ships, and that obviously had not been achieved. Furthermore, the Kaiser's navy had fallen behind in other areas, such as submarines. By 1914, Britain had 88 submarines; the French owned 76; the United States had 32; and the Kaiserreich had produced only 22, the bulk of which were obsolete.[40]

Several opportunities for formal arms-control agreements between Germany and Britain arose between 1906 and 1912; these included the 1907 Hague conference, British efforts to negotiate an understanding from 1908 to 1911, and the Haldane mission of 1912.[41] However, as is so often the case when one party senses a better bargain can be had by holding out, no formal agreement was reached. Perhaps more importantly, Germany's preoccupation with coercing Britain into a partnership left her without an ally capable of helping her close the naval gap.

The first arms race of the twentieth century was truly modern in character and global in scope. The arms race itself was a by-product of this zero-sum game

---

[38] John H. Morrow, *German Airpower in World War I* (Lincoln, 1982), 7.
[39] Paul M. Kennedy, *The Rise of Anglo-German Antagonism, 1860-1914* (London, 1987).
[40] Robert Hutchinson, *Jane's Submarines: War Beneath the Waves from 1776 to the Present Day* (New York, 2005).
[41] John H. Maurer, "Arms Control and the Anglo-German Naval Race before World War I: Lessons for Today?" Political Science Quarterly 112 (1997), 285-306.

mentality, and the individual armaments programs of each power were but instruments in the service of active political and diplomatic maneuvering, which both used and misused the twin strategies of deterrence and coercion, as the main examples above demonstrate.

Conclusions

The dynamics of the naval arms race point to the following considerations regarding strategies of deterrence and coercive diplomacy. First, deterrence is not likely to preserve peace over the long run (meaning decades rather than years) without an active commitment by both sides to avoid a general conflict. This is because political, economic, and technological changes are likely to occur over the long-term that will shift the balance of power in favor of one party or the other. If the shift is too great, the original premises for deterrence will have been rendered obsolete, and new ones will need to be negotiated. A shared commitment to avoid war was essentially absent in the decades before 1914. War may not have been aggressively sought; surely the Kaiser did not seek it. He passed up on the opportunity to attack France in 1905, while Russia was too weak from the Russo-Japanese War to mount a serious counterattack in the east. Nonetheless, the use of military force as a form of intimidation, particularly during the Moroccan crises (1905, 1911), clearly showed that peace and stability were not priorities. Rather, the guiding objective was influence or control.

Second, changes in economic capacity, technological development, or political resolve will cause shifts in any balance of power, thereby undermining prospects for successful deterrence. From 1890 onward, Great Britain remained the dominant military power at sea. Nonetheless, by 1913, the second, third, and fourth ranked naval powers had changed, making for a different constellation of power relationships in Europe and Asia. Germany was still the dominant land-power, but France led the way in air power, which was still an underdeveloped weapon. This uneven distribution and reordering of military power was due not only to increased economic growth, but also to the second- and third-order effects of the Industrial Revolution. Modern states could develop armaments programs much more rapidly, and the use of such capacities as political instruments became common practice.

United States soldiers in Verdun, World War I

Ernst Barlach, "Der Rächer" ("The Avenger")

Eurasia's Emerging Geopolitics: Back to 1914?

Artyom Lukin and Andrey Gubin

Abstract:

This chapter explores the risks of a major, or "world," war starting in Asia and engulfing much of Eurasia, drawing upon the analogies from the pre-WWI international system. Whereas the first two world wars broke out in Europe and had it as their main battlefield, WWIII, if it is not avoided, will most probably erupt in the Asia-Pacific. While a great-power war is hardly probable now and in the near future, it can be made more likely if Eurasia slides into hostile alliance politics and splits into the U.S.-centered and China-dominated camps, with Moscow becoming an ally of Beijing.

Key words: Eurasia, geopolitics, international security, Russia, China, the United States, world war.

Introduction

This chapter aims to explore the risks of a major, or "world," war starting in Asia and engulfing much of Eurasia, drawing upon the analogies and lessons from the pre-World War I international system. Whereas the first two world wars broke out in Europe and had it as their main battle field, World War III, if it is not avoided, will most probably erupt in the Asia-Pacific.

A world war is understood as a lengthy (lasting at least one year) military conflict, having as its principal theater one of the key regions of the world, in which at least two great powers confront one another in active hostilities, while many other major and lesser states are directly or indirectly involved. A world war is likely to feature a confrontation of two camps, led by great powers and possessing roughly comparable strategic resources such that one side will not easily and swiftly prevail over the other. Such a war, even if it is mostly limited to one geographic area, will have significant global repercussions, essentially ending the preceding international order.

The chapter begins with identifying alarming parallels between pre-WWI Europe and modern Asia. It proceeds to review Asia's principal rivalries and flashpoints, finding that there is a low likelihood of a major war in Asia for at least the next few years. However, it goes on to argue that the risk of war can grow if Eurasia splits into the U.S.-centered and China-dominated camps, with Moscow becoming a great-power ally of Beijing, akin to the bond Austria-Hungary had with Wilhelmine Germany. It draws up a hypothetical scenario of the Third World War that could be initiated along the lines of WWI, but whose conduct will be very different from the big wars of the twentieth century. In conclusion, it emphasizes the increasing risk of Eurasia sliding into hostile alliance politics and suggests a Eurasian concert as a way to build a stable multipolar order.

Europe's Past and Asia's Present: Troubling Parallels

Quite a few scholars have found similarities between what was taking place in Europe before World War I and what we are now witnessing in Asia. As Barry Buzan and Ole Waever argued, "Asia is not unlike nineteenth century Europe,"[1] while Aaron Friedberg claimed that "Europe's past could be Asia's future," with Asia most likely to be the global "cockpit of great power conflict."[2] Even politicians cannot resist the temptation of drawing historical parallels, with Japan's Prime Minister Shinzo Abe declaring that the increasing tensions between China and Japan were similar to the competition between Germany and Britain before World War I.[3]

It is hard to deny that there is an array of parallels between the pre-World War I Europe and the contemporary Asia:

- **Mutual animosities and hatreds rooted in the not-so-distant history.** European antagonisms to a large extent stemmed from historical traumas and grievances such as the French desire for

---

[1] Barry Buzan and Ole Waever, *Regions and Powers: The Structure of International Security* (Cambridge: Cambridge University Press 2003), 174.

[2] Aaron L. Friedberg, "Ripe for Rivalry: Prospects for Peace in a Multipolar Asia," *International Security*. 18/3 (Winter 1993-4), 7.

[3] Jane Perlez, "Japan's Leader Compares Strain With China to Germany and Britain in 1914," *The New York Times*, January 23, 2014,
<http://www.nytimes.com/2014/01/24/world/asia/japans-leader-compares-strain-with-china-to-germany-and-britain-in-1914.html?src=rechp&_r=0>.

revanche over Germany to regain Alsace-Lorraine. Nowadays, Asian rivalries are fueled by very similar grudges and disagreements, such as Sino-Japanese, Sino-Indian, Korean-Japanese, and Russo-Japanese disputes.

- **Alliance entrapment.** The outbreak of Europe's Great War was helped by the existence of rigid alliance arrangements, whereby great powers were obliged to come to the rescue of their allies and clients, thus risking turning a bilateral conflict into general war. Modern Asia features the hub-and-spoke system of the U.S.-led alliances, committing Washington to the defense of its junior partners.

- **The rising tide of nationalism.** Resembling Europe's past, Asia today is characterized by high-intensity nationalist sentiments. Most states in Asia, including China, Japan, and both Koreas, are ethnic nation-states. As Europe learned the hard way, ethnic nation-making has been conducive to domestic and international conflict in a number of ways, in particular exacerbating racially-based animosities between exclusively ethnic nation-states.[4] Ethno-nationalism "corresponds to some enduring propensities of the human spirit that are heightened by the processes of modern state creation."[5] Much of Asia is now passing through exactly that stage of modern nation-building. Modernization, bringing with it state centralization, industrialization, urbanization, mass education, and the spread of mass media, has transformed the basic characteristics of the Asian populace, making it susceptible to virulent chauvinism. For example, the mass consciousness of the European citizenry exactly was shaped by the newly invented mass circulation press, which often espoused nationalistic and imperialistic views. Today, internet media like the Chinese microblogging website *Weibo* have become a breeding ground for nationalistic feelings, particularly among the younger generations.

- **The dominance of the Westphalian state.** Nationalism is closely related to the Westphalian type of international order, which rests on sovereign nation-states. Whereas in the West the nationalistic nation-state with unbounded sovereignty seems to have run its course and is

---

[4] Muthiah Alagappa, *Nation Making in Asia: From Ethnic to Civic Nations?* (Institute of Strategic and International Studies Malaysia 2012), <www.isis.org.my>, 6.
[5] Jerry Z. Muller, "Us and Them: The Enduring Power of Ethnic Nationalism," in *The Clash of Civilizations: The Debate* (New York: Council on Foreign Relations 2010), 100-119.

viewed by many as an anachronism to be overcome, in Asia it may be well in its prime. As Muthiah Alagappa observes, "among the countries in the world it is the Asian states that most closely approximate the Westphalian state."[6] He is echoed by Henry Kissinger: in Asia, "[t]he principles of sovereignty prevail, more so than on their continent of origin."[7] The Westphalian system of sovereign nation-states, in conjunction with the phenomenon of mass nationalism, leads to intensified conflicts in the international arena, as exemplified by the First and Second World Wars that were unleashed by the European states in the age of modernity. Asia provides similar examples in China and India, which had peacefully coexisted for more than two thousand years but became strategic adversaries once they started building modern nation-states. This is also the case in the Sino-Japanese relationship, which had been generally pacific until the late nineteenth century, when Japanese and Chinese modernization/nation-building projects went at loggerheads.

- **The concentration of great powers.** Just like Europe in its heyday, today's Asia boasts a constellation of great powers. Before the First World War, Europe had as many as six great powers vying for control of the continent: Russia, England, France, Austria-Hungary, Germany, and Italy. Asia currently has five: China, Japan, India, Russia, and the US.[8] The fact that so many of Asia's constituent units either already hold great power mantles or strongly aspire for major power status (Korea, Pakistan, probably Indonesia and Vietnam) makes for instability, fuelling contests among the powers' egos.

- **The power shifts and dissatisfaction with status quo.** In the late nineteenth century, Europe's equilibrium was disrupted by the surge in German power. The rising German Empire clamored for its "place in the sun," rapidly moving to become the pre-eminent continental power while undercutting Britain's positions in world trade and challenging the Royal Navy's supremacy. Today, China appears, to many, very much

---

[6] Muthiah Alagappa, "Constructing Security Order in Asia," in Muthiah Alagappa (ed.), *Asian Security Order: Instrumental and Normative Features* (Stanford: Stanford University Press 2003), 87.
[7] Henry Kissinger, *On China* (New York: The Penguin Press 2011), 527.
[8] The US, albeit not an Asian power geographically, is so intimately entangled in its affairs that it can be counted as one of Asia's crucial players. This distinguishes the current US position in Asia from the pre-World War I Europe, where the US was an external and largely detached actor.

like Wilhelmine Germany: an economic juggernaut, with its growing geo-political ambitions backed up by the rising military capabilities. Just like Imperial Germany, the People's Republic of China is perceived by many as a revisionist and assertive power. Just like Germany, positioned in the middle of Europe, China occupies the central place on the Asian continent, giving it inherent geostrategic advantages of being in a pivotal position but at the same time rendering it vulnerable to potential strategic encirclement and multi-front wars.

Dissatisfaction with the status quo does not only pertain to China. Other great powers in Asia, except for the US, are more or less unsatisfied with their current status in the international system. This is particularly true of Japan, India, and Russia.[9] This makes another parallel with pre-Great War Europe, where all the major players, save Great Britain, sought changes to the existing order to suit their various demands.

- **Conflict triggers.** World War I was ignited by the apparently insignificant contestation in the Balkan Peninsula between Austria-Hungary and Serbia. In today's Asia, there are a number of such potential war triggers relating to comparatively minor issues like the Senkakus, the Spratlys, and the border dispute in the Himalayas.

- **Race for space.** The late 19th century and the early 20th century was an era of unbridled imperialism, with great powers scrambling for colonies in Africa and the Asia-Pacific. The battle for colonial possessions did much to poison the relations among the European powers. The colonial struggle is no more, but we are now witnessing another race for geopolitical space, this time manifested in the competition for control over the Arctic and global maritime "commons." This is a competition where Asian powers, particularly China, are getting increasingly involved.[10]

- **Naval buildup.** The dynamics of naval capabilities of the principal players will serve as a key indicator of their determination to seek, or defend, domination in the Indo-Pacific. Some analysts predict that China is destined to grow into a naval power, and, as an initial step,

---

[9] Alagappa, "Constructing Security Order in Asia."
[10] Shannon Tiezzi, "China Sees Arctic Race Heating Up," *The Diplomat*, February 21, 2014, <http://thediplomat.com/2014/02/china-sees-arctic-race-heating-up/>.

Beijing would try to establish control over the South China Sea.[11] Chinese naval buildup and the American response cannot yet be compared to the grand Anglo-German naval race that became one of the causes of World War I. China's main objective is not to dethrone America from the position of global maritime supremacy, but rather to achieve strategic dominance within the so-called "first island chain." However, according to some assessments, China might try to extend its naval reach up to the Hawaii Islands after 2020.[12] Such a move would inevitably trigger an American response and significantly raise Sino-US tensions.

- **Economic interdependence.** Before World War I, as now, there was a remarkable expansion in global trade and investment.[13] Economic interdependence was high and rising, including among the future belligerents. The economic relationship between Britain and Germany was particularly strong. Britain was the leading market for German exports, while Britain was a close second to the US as Germany's most important bilateral trade partner in 1913.[14]

In a very similar vein, the current Sino-American commercial relationship has become one of the mainstays of the global economy, with the bilateral trade topping half a trillion dollars. China is now the US's second-largest trade partner and its biggest source of imports. In addition, China is the largest holder of the US public debt. China is also the number one trade partner for Japan, Russia, North and South Korea, ASEAN countries, and India.

---

[11] Robert Kaplan. "The South China Sea Is the Future of Conflict," Foreign Policy September/October 2011, <http://www.foreignpolicy.com/articles/2011/08/15/the_south_china_sea_is_the_future_of_conflict>.

[12] Alexei Arbatov, "Aziatsko-tikhookeenskaya strategicheskaya panorama stremitel'no menyaetsya," Nezavisimoye Voyennoye Obozreniye, February 21, 2014, <http://nvo.ng.ru/realty/2014-02-21/1_asia.html>.

[13] Margaret MacMillan, "The Rhyme of History: Lessons of the Great War," Brookings, December 14, 2013, <http://www.brookings.edu/research/essays/2013/rhyme-of-history-print>.

[14] Paul A.Papayoanou, "Interdependence, Institutions, and the Balance of Power: Britain, Germany, and World War I," International Security 20/4 (Spring 1996), 42-76.

World War I proved beyond doubt that high economic interdependence is not nearly enough to secure peace, so it would be another "great illusion" to trust that the Asia-Pacific's dense web of trade and investment can avert war.

Asia's Constellation of Flashpoints: Can They Escalate to a Big War?

This section briefly assesses Asia's principal antagonisms and flashpoints. They are linked by the striking fact that China is involved in each one of them, whether directly or indirectly.

US-Chinese rivalry

Resurgent China regards East Asia as its natural sphere of influence and America as the only force truly able to hamper its geopolitical aspirations.[15] So far, America's behavior towards China can be characterized as hedging, or "soft" containment ("contagement"), as distinguished from the "hard" containment applied to the Soviet Union and, until the early 1970s, to communist China itself. Washington seems to have not *as yet* identified Beijing as a clear and present danger that needs to be dealt with at all costs. Here some analogies can be drawn from how Britain perceived the German challenge before World War I: London's concerns about Berlin grew into existential anxiety only after it became clear that, firstly, Germany had become the preponderant force in the continental Europe, which could not possibly be balanced by the other continental powers combined, and, secondly, Germany had embarked on an ambitious naval program threatening the Royal Navy supremacy.

In a similar fashion, the US will likely activate "hard" containment of China if: 1) China comes within close reach of Asian dominance, with other Asian powers being unable to collectively pose an effective counterweight; 2) China acquires formidable blue-water assets capable of challenging the US Navy's dominance in the Pacific. Either one of these conditions or both of them

---

[15] Wang Yizhou, "Opportunities and Challenges for China's New Leaders in Building Mutual Trust with the World," *Global Asia* Fall 2013, 34.

together are likely to serve as the red line for the US, signaling the beginning of full-blown antagonism.

Sino-Japanese antagonism

While a US-Chinese rivalry is largely subject to description in terms of the balance of power theory and offers a typical case study of a dominating power responding to the emergence of a powerful contender, the Sino-Japanese relationship presents a much more complex mix, with emotions seemingly prevailing over geostrategic calculations. The Sino-Japanese dyad is now in many ways reminiscent of Franco-German antagonism after the Franco-Prussian War of 1870-71.

Today's disputes between China and Japan are focused on the sovereignty of the Senkaku (Diaoyu) Islands in the East China Sea. Almost inconceivable several years ago, a military clash over several uninhabited islets may become a reality.[16] Were there only the two parties to the conflict (Beijing and Tokyo), China would be favored to prevail over Japan, given its numerical naval and air superiority. However, if the US gets directly involved, China will almost certainly be defeated by the combined forces of the US-Japanese alliance, provided the clash occurs now or in the next few years.[17]

The debacle on the battlefield could give rise to public unrest against the Communist Party rule, followed by a radical transformation of the regime and ascension of new political forces.[18] The scenario might be similar to Argentina's fate after its defeat in the Falklands War, when mass protests against the military rule broke out, ending the junta. This is one more reason

---

[16] Hugh White, "Caught in a bind that threatens an Asian war nobody wants," *The Sydney Morning Herald*, December 26, 2012,
<http://www.smh.com.au/opinion/politics/caught-in-a-bind-that-threatens-an-asian-war-nobody-wants-20121225-2bv38.html>.

[17] Andrey Gubin and Artyom Lukin, "Warring in North East Asia: Possible Scenarios," *Russian International Affairs Council*, May 28, 2013,
<http://russiancouncil.ru/en/inner/?id_4=1876#top>.

[18] These new forces replacing the Communist Party might be more democratic but no less nationalistic.

why the Chinese leaders are going to be extremely cautious in taking any substantial military moves in the East China Sea.[19]

The Korean Peninsula

While theoretically possible, a major war on the Korean Peninsula is hardly likely, as both sides remember the no-win experience of 1950-1953. They realize that a new conflict would carry momentous risks for both, including the annihilation of the 10-million-strong city of Seoul in the South and the Kim dynasty in the North. The Korean Peninsula has acquired a stable system of mutual containment propped up on one hand by America's military presence and nuclear guarantees to the South[20] and on the other hand by North Korea's nuclear missile arsenal and Beijing's allied obligations to Pyongyang. Both sides seem to recognize the lines that cannot be crossed. Even if war breaks out on the Peninsula, it is highly unlikely to spread beyond the territory of the two Koreas.

The Taiwan problem

Just a decade ago, the Taiwan problem was viewed as the most probable source of a major war in the Asia-Pacific, in which China would be pitted against the US. This has now changed. The Taiwan question still exists, but the likelihood of a crisis in the Straits leading to a great-power war has considerably diminished. It seems that American commitments to Taiwan's defense are becoming ever more ambiguous and tenuous. Given remarkable quantitative and qualitative increases in China's forces in the Western Pacific, would the US risk a war over an entity that Washington itself officially recognizes a part of the PRC?

---

[19] Jonathan D. Pollack, "Is China preparing for a 'short, sharp war' against Japan?" East Asia Forum, March 24, 2014, <http://www.eastasiaforum.org/2014/03/24/is-china-preparing-for-a-short-sharp-war-against-japan/>.

[20] William Wieninger, "Extended Deterrence on the Korean Peninsula: Stability in an Age of Global Nuclear Reductions, Maturing Missile Defenses, and DPRK Provocations," *Korea Review* 1/2 (December 2011), 132-148.

There are growing calls within the US to renounce the long-held "vision of Taiwan as a militarized base within the US strategic orbit."[21] Then Beijing would basically have the island to itself. The much-feared Taiwan crisis still may happen if Beijing decides to resort to force to reunite with the island after all, but it is unlikely to draw in the US and its allies militarily.

Indian-Chinese rivalry

Comparisons with the pre-World War I Franco-German rivalry may be even more appropriate in the case of the Sino-Indian dyad than the Sino-Japanese feud. Just like Germany and France in 1870-71, India and China fought a bloody war in 1962, in which India was humiliatingly routed, had its territory seized, and has not yet come to terms with the outcome of that defeat.

Both nations "aspire to the same things at the same time on the same continental landmass and its adjoining waters."[22] The Sino-Indian rivalry has many particular dimensions, each of which may be manageable on its own, but in combination they create quite a combustible mix. That said, a major war between China and India is currently highly unlikely for several reasons. First, the level of hostility that the Chinese harbor towards India is nowhere near the degree of enmity they display towards Japan. It is Tokyo, not New Delhi, that is Beijing's number one foe in Asia. Second, any hostilities going beyond a short and localized border clash would involve the risks of escalation up to the point of nuclear exchanges. Third, China's most important interests lie in the Western Pacific and Southeast Asia rather than in South Asia. Fourth, India strives to avoid angering China too much. In particular, there is only so far that New Delhi is prepared to go in constructing ententes with Washington[23] and Tokyo.[24] Thus far, India continues its

---

[21] See: Bruce Gilley, "Not So Dire Straits," *Foreign Affairs* January/February 2010, 44-60.
[22] Mohan Malik, *China and India: Great Power Rivals* (Boulder: First Forum Press 2011), 9.
[23] Sourabh Gupta, "The US Pivot and India's Look East," *East Asia Forum*, June 20, 2012,
<http://www.eastasiaforum.org/2012/06/20/the-us-pivot-and-india-s-look-east/>.
[24] The New York Times, "United Against China?" January 30, 2014, <http://www.nytimes.com/2014/01/31/opinion/united-against-china.html?hpw&rref=opinion>.

traditional course of "strategic independence" and definitely does not want to be seen as part of a US-led anti-China coalition.[25]

Indian-Pakistani antagonism

Although the relations between New Delhi and Islamabad remain tense, the probability of a major war is low. This is partly due to mutual nuclear deterrence, India and Pakistan both being nuclear-armed states. Moreover, the de facto alliance with China provides Islamabad with extra security guarantees. There is a high likelihood that China would intervene and open a second front in the Himalayas if, in the case of a major conflict, Pakistan proves unable to resist Indian forces and finds itself on the verge of total collapse. This is dictated by hefty strategic stakes that China has in Pakistan's continued existence.[26] China's mission as Pakistan's main protector is not unlike the role it plays on the Korean Peninsula, shielding the DPRK from the US-RoK alliance. One is tempted to draw comparisons with Wilhelmine Germany, which propped up its weaker allies – Austria-Hungary and the Ottoman Empire.

The South China Sea disputes

The Philippine President Benigno Aquino went so far as to draw parallels between China's assertiveness in the South China Sea and Hitler's demands for Czech land in 1938.[27] Comparing the PRC to Nazi Germany and the Philippines to hapless Czechoslovakia may be an overstatement. Rather than invoking the images of World War II, analogies with World War I appear to be more apt in this case. As the Balkans were at that time the space populated by small states where great powers (Austria-Hungary allied with Germany vs. Russia allied with France) competed with one another for geopolitical influence, the South China Sea is rapidly becoming an arena for

---

[25] Sumit Ganguly, "Think Again: India's rise," *Foreign Policy*, July 5, 2012, <http://www.foreignpolicy.com/articles/2012/07/05/think_again_india_s_rise?page=full>.
[26] Malik, *China and India: Great Power Rivals*, 173.
[27] Keith Bradsher, "Philippine Leader Sounds Alarm on China," *The New York Times*, February 5, 2014,
<http://www.nytimes.com/2014/02/06/world/asia/philippines.html?ref=asia&_r=0>.

the US-China strategic rivalry. Although not a claimant in the maritime controversies, Washington has taken a clear position against China and on the side of the ASEAN claimant-states,[28] encouraging them to stand up to Beijing and seeking to consolidate ASEAN on an anti-Chinese basis.[29]

One more similarity between the Balkans and the South China Sea controversies lies in what Jean-Marc Blanchard calls "adolescence of states." An adolescent state is one that is growing rapidly, unsure of its identity, has not adopted mature behaviors, and is excessively concerned with its domain and status. The adverse consequences include an intense quest for resources, a search for new identities and the protection of old ones, and often uncoordinated and erratic behavior.[30] The competitors in the Balkans, both the small Balkan nations and the great powers (Russia, Germany, Austria-Hungary), had pronounced features of an adolescent state, not unlike the current rivals in the South China Sea: a rapidly growing China, groping for a great power identity, and ASEAN countries, being in the midst of nation-building projects.

Rising passions in the South China Sea notwithstanding, there is low risk of a major militarized conflagration. Washington has made it clear that it has no intention to get involved militarily.[31] Therefore, if China chooses to use force to assert its maritime claims in the South China Sea, it will swiftly and easily prevail over its much weaker rivals without fearing a US naval response. However, for the time being, Beijing may be constrained from taking full advantage of its military preponderance, being aware that such a move could mobilize and unite ASEAN against China and play to US strategic interests.

---

[28] Mark J. Valencia, "The South China Sea Disputes," *Global Asia* Fall 2012, 56-73.

[29] Evgeny Kanaev, "ASEAN and the Code of Conduct of Parties in the South China Sea," Russian International Affairs Council, May 21, 2013, <http://russiancouncil.ru/en/inner/?id_4=1853#top>.

[30] Jean-Marc Blanchard, "Maritime Issues in Asia: the problem of adolescence," in Muthiah Alagappa (ed.), *Asian Security Order: Instrumental and Normative Features* (Stanford: Stanford University Press 2003), 426 (424-457).

[31] Rommel C. Banlaoi, "US-Philippines Alliance," in Carl Baker and Brad Glosserman (eds.), *Doing More and Expecting Less: The Future of US Alliances in the Asia Pacific* (Pacific Forum CSIS, January 2013), 62.

Why There Will Not Be a Major War in Asia Anytime Soon

To many, the current security situation in the East Asian seas – with competing sovereignty claims, the rise of nationalism among both major and lesser countries, and great power involvement – "increasingly resembles a 21st-century maritime redux of the Balkans a century ago – a tinderbox on water."[32] This, however, does not necessarily mean that Asia is on the verge of a major war. There are strong grounds to expect that, at least within the next ten years, a big conflagration is almost out of the question. If a major war is to break out in Asia, it will most likely be initiated by the principal revisionist power, China.[33] Yet China does not want war – primarily because Beijing knows that the odds are not on its side.

First, despite the double-digit annual growth in its defense budgets, China's military still significantly lags behind the US's. It will take China fifteen to twenty years to attain parity or near-parity with the US-Japanese allied forces in the East Asian littoral.[34] It is not until 2020 that the PLA is going to complete the modernization programs designed to put it on par with the world's most advanced military forces.[35]

Second, for all the talk of *mutual* interdependence, China depends on America much more than the other way round. China is still critically reliant on the US and its allies, the EU and Japan, as its principal export markets and sources of advanced technologies and know-how. Overall, China's dependence on international markets is very high, with the trade-to-GDP ratio

---

[32] Kevin Rudd, "A Maritime Balkans of the 21st Century?" Foreign Policy, January 30, 2013, <http://www.foreignpolicy.com/articles/2013/01/30/a_maritime_balkans_of_the_21st_century_east_asia>.

[33] Of course, there is also a hypothetical possibility of a preventive war started by the incumbent hegemonic power, the US, in order to take out China before it becomes too strong. However, such a scenario has a low probability. It is somewhat more likely that the US will resort to geo-economic strangling of Beijing, aiming to restrain China's access to international markets and thus limiting its GDP growth. (Edward Luttwak, *The Rise of China vs. the Logic of Strategy* (Cambridge, MA: The Belkhap Press of Harvard University Press 2012)).

[34] Michael Swaine, Mike Mochizuki, Michael Brown, et al., "China's Military and the US-Japan Alliance in 2030: a strategic net assessment," Carnegie Endowment for International Peace, May 2013, <http://carnegieendowment.org/2013/05/03/china-s-military-and-u.s.-japan-alliance-in-2030-strategic-net-assessment/g1wh>.

[35] Vasily Kashin, "Evolyutsiya Voyennoy Politiki Kitaya," *Eksport Vooruzheny* November 2012, 6-14.

standing at 53 percent.[36] China imports many vital raw materials, such as oil and iron ore. As most of its commodity imports are shipped by sea, China would be extremely vulnerable to a naval blockade, which is likely to be mounted by the US in the case of a major conflict.[37] Both for economic and strategic reasons, the Chinese government pursues policies to reduce the country's reliance on foreign markets, trying to shift from an export-oriented model to domestic sources of growth. It is also making efforts to secure raw materials in its contiguous countries and regions like Central Asia, Russia, or Burma, so as to reduce dependence on seaborne shipments. However, at least for the next 15 to 20 years, China's dependency on the Western-dominated global economic system is going to stay very significant.

Third, even if China becomes, as widely predicted, the number one economy and manages to significantly reduce, or perhaps altogether eliminate, the military gap with the US, this will not be sufficient to mount a viable challenge to the American hegemony, for China would have to confront not the US alone but the US-led bloc including, among others, Japan, the EU, Australia, and perhaps India. Thus China needs at least one major-power ally. Beijing currently has just one formal ally, North Korea, while Pakistan can be viewed as something of a de facto ally, at least vis-à-vis India. Although valuable to China, these countries can hardly be regarded as huge strategic assets. China lacks a dependable ally of a truly great power standing. The only plausible candidate is Russia. The northern neighbor's strategic depth, huge natural resources, military power, and pockets of scientific and technological prowess all could be significant force multipliers for China. Whether China dares to pose a serious challenge to the US will, to a large extent, hinge upon Beijing and Moscow forming a geopolitical bloc, which is also going to take some time.

The bottom line is that, over the next 15 to 20 years, a major war in Asia is highly unlikely. Even though the current flashpoints in Asia may exhibit many similarities to the pre-World War I situation, they lack a critical ingredient to make them truly explosive: there are no rival alliances of comparable strength, while China alone is hardly able to confront the reigning

---

[36] World Trade Organization, "WTO: China country profile,"
<http://stat.wto.org/CountryProfile/WSDBCountryPFView.aspx?Country=CN&>.

[37] Sean Mirski, "Stranglehold: The Context, Conduct and Consequences of an American Naval Blockade of China," *Journal of Strategic Studies,* February 12, 2013, DOI: 10.1080/01402390.2012.743885,
<http://dx.doi.org/10.1080/01402390.2012.743885>.

superpower. However, around 2030 the balance is bound to undergo considerable changes if China is successful in: 1) closing military gap with the US; 2) making its economy less reliant on the Western markets and overseas raw resources; and 3) striking an alliance with one or more major powers.

Towards a Eurasian Bloc: Will Russia Be China's Austria-Hungary?

As noted above, China's own power base, even when developed to its full capacity, will be insufficient to compete for geopolitical primacy with the combined might of the US and its allies. The only realistic option for Beijing to substantially augment its power is through external balancing; that is, by allying with another major player. The only great power potentially available for such an alliance is Russia.

If Sino-American rivalry goes from its currently more or less subdued mode to an open clash, Russia would find itself in a pivotal position.[38] Thus, even short of an alliance, good relations with Russia give China huge strategic benefits. First and foremost, it provides Beijing with "a stable strategic rear area."[39] With Moscow as a close friend, China can be confident about the security of its northern borders and can count on an unimpeded access to Russia's natural resources. Thus, Beijing becomes much less vulnerable to naval blockades that the US and its maritime allies are sure to use against China in the case of a serious confrontation. In an American blockade of China, Russia will be the most important "swing state" and "could tip the balance of a blockade in favor of either China or the United States."[40]

Should they form an entente, Moscow and Beijing could have Central Asia, as well as Mongolia, to themselves, effectively shutting out all external powers from the heart of Eurasia. Alliance with Moscow would also put Russia's military-industrial complex and vast Eurasian military infrastructure in Beijing's service. What might ultimately emerge is a Eurasian league, which, in controlling the continental heartland, would be reminiscent of the

---

[38] Edward Luttwak, *The Rise of China vs. the Logic of Strategy*, 141-2.
[39] Aaron L. Friedberg, *A Contest for Supremacy: China, America, and the Struggle for Mastery in Asia* (New York: W. W. Norton & Company 2012).
[40] Sean Mirski, "Stranglehold: The Context, Conduct and Consequences of an American Naval Blockade of China," 10-11.

WWI Central Powers (Mittelmächte) alliance as well as Karl Haushofer's anti-Western "continental bloc" of Germany, the Soviet Union, and Japan.[41] That could be a bilateral alliance or a multilateral pact, possibly based on the Shanghai Cooperation Organization framework.

There is a strong tendency in the West to underestimate the potential for Russo-Chinese rapprochement. Sino-Russian strategic partnership is often portrayed as an "axis of convenience"[42] founded on a shaky basis. Moscow, the argument goes, will be loath to the idea of an alliance with Beijing because it distrusts and fears the rising China.[43] The main problem with such thinking is that the US-led West is seen by Moscow as a much bigger threat than China.[44] The consensus in the Kremlin is that, for at least the next 20 years, China will not pose a threat to Russia, Beijing's and Moscow's common foe being the US.[45] As Dmitri Trenin observes, the Russia-China bond "is solid, for it is based on fundamental national interests regarding the world order as both the Russian and Chinese governments would prefer to see it."[46]

It would not be accurate to describe the Russo-Chinese strategic partnership as an alliance yet, but the relationship is certainly growing stronger. In particular, Russia and China have been increasing the extent of their joint military exercises. For example, in July 2013, they conducted naval drills in the Sea of Japan, touted by Beijing as the country's "single biggest deployment of military force in any joint foreign exercise."[47] Russia recently

---

[41] The leading Nazi geopolitician Karl Haushofer put this idea forward in 1940. The concept is almost forgotten in the West, but is well known, and increasingly popular, within Russia's strategic community.

[42] Bobo Lo, *Axis of Convenience: Moscow, Beijing, and the New Geopolitics* (Brookings Institution Press 2008).

[43] There is also a minority view in the West that China and Russia could well form a durable alliance. See: Gordon G. Chang, "China and Russia: An Axis of Weak States," World Affairs March/April 2014, <http://www.worldaffairsjournal.org/article/china-and-russia-axis-of-weak-states>.

[44] Artyom Lukin, "Russia: between the US and China," East Asia Forum, July 24, 2012, <http://www.eastasiaforum.org/2012/07/24/russia-between-the-us-and-china-2/>.

[45] Remarks by Leonid Reshetnikov, Director of the Russian Institute for Strategic Studies (a think tank under the Russian President), Roundtable at Far Eastern Federal University, Vladivostok, February 2014 (personal notes).

[46] Dmitri Trenin, "Russia and the Rise of Asia," *Carnegie Moscow Center*, November 2013, <carnegie.ru>, 6.

[47] Chang Ching, "Overrated Significance of the Sino-Russia 'Joint-Sea 2013' Exercise?" *Pacific Forum CSIS*, August 6, 2013, <http://csis.org/publication/pacnet-61-overrated-significance-sino-russia-joint-sea-2013-exercise>.

started to display more willingness to sell its most advanced weapons to China.[48] Signed in May 2014, the 30-year gas mega-deal between Gazprom and CNPC also carries significant strategic overtones. Regarding mutual perceptions, Russia is the most positively viewed major power in China,[49] while the majority of Russians hold favorable opinions of China.[50]

There are rising calls among the expert community in both countries to upgrade the partnership to a full-scale alliance.[51] In May 2014, China's first blue book on national security, produced by the Chinese Institutes of Contemporary International Relations, stated that China should consider forming an "alliance with Russia."[52]

The Ukraine crisis of 2014 may well become a tipping point that seals the fate of Eurasian alignments. The Western push to punish and isolate Russia over its actions in Ukraine is likely to draw Moscow closer to Beijing, which, tellingly, has taken a stance of benevolent neutrality towards the Kremlin's takeover of Crimea.[53] One may suspect that in exchange, Beijing would

---

[48] Stephen Blank, "Shared Threat Perceptions Begin Renewal of Sino-Russian Arms Trade," *Jamestown Foundation*, February 15, 2013, <http://www.jamestown.org/single/?no_cache=1&tx_ttnews%5Btt_news%5D=40464 >; Ivan Safronov. "Moskva Podelitsya 'Triumfom' s Pekinom," March 28, 2014, *Kommersant*, <http://www.kommersant.ru/doc/2439430>.

[49] Pew Research Center, "China and the World," October 16, 2012, <http://www.pewglobal.org/2012/10/16/chapter-2-china-and-the-world/>.

[50] *Transatlantic Trends. Key Findings 2012*, German Marshall Fund of the United States, <http://trends.gmfus.org/transatlantic-trends/>.

[51] For Chinese views arguing in favor of the alliance with Russia, see, for example, Yan Xuetong, "The Weakening of the Unipolar Configuration," in Mark Leonard (ed.) *China 3.0* (London: European Council on Foreign Relations, November 2012), <http://ecfr.eu/page/-/ECFR66_CHINA_30_final.pdf>, 112-119; *Global Times*, "US Actions Make China-Russia Alliance Appealing," January 20, 2012, <http://english.peopledaily.com.cn/90780/7710844.html>; Dai Xu, "Kitayu i Rossii sledueyet sozdat' Evraziyskiy Alyans," *People's Daily* (Russian-language edition), January 30, 2012, <http://russian.people.com.cn/95181/7714612.html>. For a Russian view supporting the alliance with China, see Yuri Tavrovski, "Zapad tolkayet Rossiyu na vostok," October 23, 2013, *Nezavisimoye Voyennoye Obozreniye*, <http://nvo.ng.ru/ideas/2013-10-23/5_geopolitics.html>.

[52] Beijing News, "Terrorism surging in China: blue paper," May 7, 2014, http://www.bjd.com.cn/10beijingnews/focus/201405/07/t20140507_6769522.html

[53] Shannon Tiezzi, "China Backs Russia on Ukraine," *The Diplomat*, 4 March 2014, <http://thediplomat.com/2014/03/china-backs-russia-on-ukraine/>.

expect from Moscow the same kind of "benevolent neutrality" regarding its assertions in East Asia and the Western Pacific.[54]

It is a cruel irony that the Ukraine crisis should have broken out the year of the hundredth anniversary of the Great War. Russia's current stance towards Ukraine is reminiscent of how, in the late 19th and early 20th centuries, Austria-Hungary felt about the Balkans, which it deemed its vital sphere of influence. The fear of losing control over the Balkans drove Austria-Hungary into the embrace of Imperial Germany, even though Vienna and Berlin had traditionally vied for control of Central Europe and fought a war in 1866. The alliance of Germany and Austria-Hungary contributed to Europe's splitting into two camps and eventually to the general war.

Could this be the model for the Sino-Russian dyad? Just like Vienna and Berlin, Moscow and Beijing have had a historically complicated relationship, but this may not preclude them forming an entente. Challenging Russia in its "Balkans" – Ukraine and the post-Soviet space generally, which the Russians characteristically call "near abroad" – the West raises the likelihood of turning Russia into a modern-day Austria-Hungary, a besieged great power seeking support from an aspiring superpower and thus becoming its junior ally. Prominent Russian analysts already talk about the possibility of Russia becoming strategically dependent on China as Beijing's junior partner.[55] In April 2014, in the midst of the Ukraine crisis, Vladimir Putin hinted that Russia might at some point consider forming a political-military alliance with China.[56]

The personalities of Russian and Chinese leaders, Putin and Xi Jinping, are going to be a major factor in deciding the fate of Russo-Chinese alignment. They are two autocratic chief executives who have concentrated in their

---

[54] Peter Ford, "China believes that the clash between Russia and the West over Ukraine will draw Moscow closer to Beijing," March 27, 2014, *The Christian Science Monitor*, <http://www.csmonitor.com/World/Asia-Pacific/2014/0327/How-US-Russia-tensions-boost-Beijing-video>.

[55] Fyodor Lukyanov, "Modifitsirovanniy Variant XIX Veka," March 18, 2014, <http://www.vz.ru/politics/2014/3/18/677533.html>. The junior status will mainly mean Russia's inferiority in its *economic* relationship with China. However, *politically* Russia will strive to remain a great power and be on a more or less equal footing with China. Moscow will recognize East Asia as China's sphere of influence, but will do so in exchange for Beijing's support of Russian privileged interests in Eastern Europe and the post-Soviet space.

[56] Vladimir Putin, *Direct line with Vladimir Putin*, April 17, 2014, <http://eng.kremlin.ru/news/7034>.

hands almost exclusive power to make foreign policy decisions.[57] Putin and Xi seem to get along quite well and share a flair for hardball realpolitik. Matched against contemporary Western leaders with underwhelming foreign policy performances, the Putin-Xi duo is going to be a formidable force. It is significant that Putin and Xi are here to stay for a long time: Putin is likely to seek, and win, re-election in 2018, while Xi will not quit until 2022 and may in fact continue to serve as China's paramount leader beyond 2022.

The international system is now at a critical juncture: US uni-polarity is waning, and the contours of the new order are taking shape. The crucial question is whether this emerging order will be one of multi-polarity and flexible balance of power or one divided into two hostile alliances. In fact, one alliance has already been in place for over sixty years. Or rather, it is the network of alliances led by Washington: NATO in the western part of Eurasia and the "hub-and-spoke" security pacts in East Asia. Is this American-centered web of alliances going to be opposed by another grouping, most probably dominated by Beijing?

In 2003, Avery Goldstein argued that since 1996, China had been pursuing a foreign policy similar to Bismarckian Germany's diplomatic strategy: "China has attempted to build a series of relationships with other major powers that enhance its attractiveness as a partner while maximizing its own leverage and flexibility by not firmly aligning with any particular state or group of states. Rather than explicitly identifying friends and enemies among principal actors on the international scene, China sought to establish partnerships with each as a way of binding their interests to China's and reducing the likelihood that any would be able to cobble together a hostile coalition…"[58]

Goldstein goes on to point out the risk: "Should China's relations with any of the major powers significantly deteriorate, especially if the international

---

[57] In Russia's case, there has never been much doubt that it is Putin who personally makes all the major foreign policy and security decisions. In China, strategic decision-making has until recently been done by the party-state collective leadership, but now Xi appears to be running the country's diplomatic and security policies on his own, with the Politburo's Standing Committee playing very little role (Jane Perlez. *Chinese Leader's One-Man Show Complicates Diplomacy.* The New York Times, July 8, 2014, http://www.nytimes.com/2014/07/09/world/asia/china-us-xi-jinpeng-washington-kerry-lew.html?ref=asia&_r=0).

[58] Avery Goldstein, "An Emerging China's Emerging Grand Strategy: a neo-Bismarckian turn?" in G. John Ikenberry and Michael Mastanduno (eds), *International Relations Theory and the Asia-Pacific* (New York: Columbia University Press 2003), 74.

system does become truly multipolar, the remaining partnerships might be reinterpreted as de facto alliances."[59]

China might not yet have abandoned this neo-Bismarckian grand strategy, but its continuation looks much less certain than a decade ago. Should Beijing pursue an alliance with Moscow, this could set in motion the strategic dynamics very similar to what Europe witnessed in the run-up to World War I, when the Franco-Russian agreements of 1891 and 1894 "marked a watershed in Europe's rush toward war" by turning the balance-of-power diplomacy rigid and ushering in a zero-sum game.[60]

Like Russia and China, India is also facing a choice of whether to enter the game of major-power alliances. India's main suitors are the US and Japan. So far, its growing strategic links with Washington and Tokyo notwithstanding, New Delhi has eschewed commitments that could entangle it in an anti-Chinese coalition. However, the Indians do not rule out the option of alignments "to meet the challenges of a hostile environment."[61]

There is a high probability that the geopolitical division into hostile alliances will be accompanied, and reinforced, by the split of the global economy into rival trading blocs, one centered on the US and the other on China. America's global economic strategy seems to aim for the construction of two mega-projects, the Trans-Pacific Partnership for the Asia-Pacific and the Trans-Atlantic Trade and Investment Partnership for the Euro-Atlantic, with Washington as the nexus. Beijing and Moscow are trying to build their own economic integration structures in the form of the Regional Comprehensive Economic Partnership and the Eurasian Economic Union, which may, within 10-20 years, merge into one organization dominated by China.

---

[59] Goldstein, "An Emerging China's Emerging Grand Strategy: a neo-Bismarckian turn?" 86.
[60] Henry Kissinger, *Diplomacy* (New York: Simon & Schuster 1994), 181-2.
[61] Deepak Kapoor, "Sino-India Border Row: is India prepared to deal with Chinese provocation?" *India Today*, May 2, 2013, <http://indiatoday.intoday.in/story/sino-india-border-row-is-india-prepared-to-deal-with-chinese-provocation/1/268947.html>.

2034: What World War III May Look Like

There is, of course, an infinite number of alternative futures. World War III erupting in Asia may not be the most probable one, yet it is not the most implausible, either. In this section, we will attempt to outline a scenario of a major military conflict breaking out in Asia and escalating to become the Third World War.

2034. China – which four years ago completed its reunification with Taiwan – is increasingly worried by the growth of India's comprehensive power. By 2030, India overtook China to become the world's most populous country. Even more significantly, India, with its much younger population and dynamic economy, has already been growing faster than China. India is vigorously modernizing its armed forces, which in a few years may present a serious challenge to China. With Indian-Chinese rivalry for primacy in Asia reaching new highs, Beijing resolves to strike first, before New Delhi has a chance to close the power gap.[62] Citing Indian meddling in Tibet and incursions across the still-not-delimited Himalayan frontier, Chinese forces go on the offensive in the border areas and hit Indian naval and air bases. The attack on India means war with Japan, as Tokyo and New Delhi concluded a mutual defense treaty in 2031 – to insure against exactly such a probable Chinese assault. Simultaneously with the attack on India, the PLA seizes the Senkakus and tries to capture the Ryukyu Islands.

In 2032, the Americans withdrew their forces from Japan, expecting that the Japan-India pact and the fact that Japan had, in 2029, become a nuclear-armed state would be sufficient to deter China. The Chinese, in turn, have made a gamble that the US, appearing to be in a newly isolationist mode, would not intervene on Japan's behalf. They prove to be wrong. After some hesitation, the US declares war against China. Two of America's Pacific allies, Australia and the Philippines, follow suit. Three NATO members – Canada, Britain, and Poland – also declare war on China and send troops to the Indo-Pacific Theater.

---

[62] This may be similar to how, in 1914, German concerns over the steady rise in Russia's strategic capabilities contributed to Berlin's decision in favor of war in the wake of the Sarajevo crisis. There was a belief among the German leadership that by 1917, Russia would complete its military modernization programs and the window of opportunity would close.

China is not alone in this war. In 2025, China, Russia, Belarus, Kazakhstan, Kyrgyzstan, Tajikistan, Turkmenistan, and Pakistan signed the Eurasian Treaty – a collective defense pact that became a political-military arm of the Shanghai Cooperation Organization. Mongolia was forced to join the pact in 2033.

Russia protects China in the north, provides it with raw materials and military hardware, and dispatches a small number of military personnel such as fighter pilots and drone operators to fight in PLA units. Apart from that, Russian direct involvement in the Indo-Pacific Theater is minimal. Moscow is mostly preoccupied with Eastern Europe, particularly Ukraine, where pro-Western forces supported by the EU and NATO have attempted to regain control over eastern and southern Ukraine which, before war in Asia broke out, had been Russia's zone of influence. Russia and the EU/NATO, while not formally in hostilities, are now embroiled in a proxy war in Ukraine.

Korea, which since 2027 has been a confederation of North and South, stays non-aligned. Southeast Asian countries (except for the Philippines) also declare their neutrality, as do African, Latin American, and Middle Eastern states.

In terms of warfare, WWIII will be vastly different from the major conflicts of the twentieth century. For one thing, the major combatants will be nuclear powers. Being aware that the actual use of atomic weapons will result in mutual extermination, the warring sides will refrain from resorting to them. That will not be unlike WWII, when the belligerents held large stockpiles of chemical weapons but did not use them for fear of retaliation. Nuclear weapons are also likely to have a moderating effect on the conduct of conventional hostilities. A state is likely to employ nuclear weapons as a last resort, particularly if its heartland is invaded or its major cities are bombarded. Understanding this, the other side may prefer not to drive the opponent into a corner. This could involve deliberately confining the main combat zones to peripheral areas, away from the most populated and industrialized regions. Furthermore, military strategists will likely remember lessons of the past: that a large offensive land war on the Asian continent is almost always a lost affair. All these considerations leave the sea, the air, and barren mountainous areas, as well as outer space and cyberspace, the principal battlegrounds for WWIII in Asia.

Another peculiarity of WWIII may be the continued functioning of diplomacy and international bodies, serving as effective channels of communications between the adversaries. Many decades of international institution-building will have proved not to be entirely in vain. Having failed to prevent war, international institutions will at least help limit its scope and temper its effects. Even trade and financial transactions between the enemies may survive to some degree, being rerouted via neutral parties like Korea, Singapore, or Turkey. This would be the ultimate proof that economic interdependence and war do not necessarily exclude each other.

Perhaps what we will witness might be termed a "world war-lite." As such it may not require total mobilization of human and material resources. In this regard, WWIII could be more similar to the Spanish Succession or Seven Years' Wars of the 18th century than the "total" world wars of the past century. The fact that the war will involve comparatively limited casualties and not necessitate complete mobilization of resources may have the unintended effect of extending it indefinitely, compared to the past wars of attrition which could only be fought for a few years because resources got rapidly exhausted. If a war does not strain societies to unbearable degrees, they may learn to live with it. Thus, could the Third World War be a Thirty or even Fifty Years' War?

That said, there will always be a risk that at some point, the "humane" low-intensity warfare with designated no-combat zones and codes of conduct could degenerate into more traditional bloodshed with heavy casualties and no restraining rules. Escalation to nuclear warfare cannot be excluded either. Whatever its outcome, this war will certainly end the world as we know it.

Conclusion

The contemporary strategic picture in Asia has a number of striking, and alarming, similarities with pre-World War I Europe. This does not mean that war is imminent. Although having many similarities with the pre-WWI situation, Asia's overlapping rivalries and flashpoints are not presently capable of generating a major war. However, if unresolved, these conflicts may explode into general war in a couple of decades.

China, the power most likely to politically and militarily challenge the US-dominated international order, will need at least another 15-20 years to modernize its armed forces, grow its GDP, and reduce its economic dependence on the West and seaborne imports of raw materials. However,

China's potential, even if realized to its maximum extent, will not be nearly enough to take on the US and its web of alliances. In terms of structural realism, China must perform external balancing in addition to internal balancing. Beijing needs at least one great power ally, which could realistically only be Russia. Therefore, China's future bid for hegemony hinges on how successful Beijing is in constructing its own alliances.

Chinese leadership may be on the verge of abandoning its strategy of non-alignment, although the final decision has yet to be made. Eurasia now resembles Europe in the early 1890s, when the configuration of rival alliances was being decided. It took Franco-Russian, Franco-British and Anglo-Russian agreements (1891-4, 1904, and 1907), plus the series of colonial and Balkan crises, to finally push Europe to war. We have not yet passed the point of no return, beyond which strategic partnerships gel into political-military alliances, but we may be fast approaching this point, which was underscored by the Ukraine crisis.

One problem is that today, as then, we lack statesmen of Bismarckian stature with strategic vision capable of perceiving the canvas of world geopolitics in its entirety and in the long-term perspective. Yet it is important to see Eurasia as a single geopolitical space, where Europe, the Middle East, Central, South, and East Asia are increasingly linked. Zbigniew Brzezinski's metaphor of Eurasia as a grand chess board[63] is now more relevant than ever.

Russia, China, and the US are the three most powerful strategic actors in Eurasia and on the world stage, and they are likely to remain so for at least the next twenty years. They constitute the most important great-power constellation in international politics. None of them is innocent, but America's policies seem especially short-sighted and provocative in that Washington tries to contain *both* Russia and China. This is what Johan Galtung calls "a coordinated pincer move" by the US and its European/Asia-Pacific allies, "aiming at the Eurasian landmass and Russia/China."[64] When the US enjoyed its "unipolar moment" in the 1990s and the first half of the 2000s, Washington could easily pursue this dual containment. Since that time, the balance of power has changed significantly. As even some prominent strategists in the US acknowledge, now America is hardly in a position to

---

[63] Zbigniew Brzezinski, *The Grand Chessboard: American Primacy and Its Geostrategic Imperatives* (New York: Basic Books 1998).
[64] Johan Galtung, *Pax Pacifica* (London: Pluto Press 2005), 56.

confront two great powers in Eurasia simultaneously.[65] However, the pincer move continues, literally pushing Russia and China together and tempting them into a fateful alliance.

A Eurasian concert of powers, borrowing some of the elements from the nineteenth-century Concert of Europe, could be one possible way to avoid a slide into the trap of hostile alliance politics and to build a stable multi-polar order. The accommodation among the US, China, and Russia must form the initial basis for a multipolar and multilateral international architecture in which other Eurasian players should also be invested and engaged. This will be an immensely difficult task to be sure, but in trying to accomplish it we will at least have the benefit of historical lessons.

Acknowledgements

The authors wish to express thanks to Andreas Herberg-Rothe, Pyotr Topychkanov, Ivan Timofeyev, Konstantin Asmolov, Ilya Kirillovsky, and Michael Rozenfeld for their valuable comments and ideas.

---

[65] John Mearsheimer, "Getting Ukraine Wrong," March 13,, 2014, *The New York Times*, http://www.nytimes.com/2014/03/14/opinion/getting-ukraine-wrong.html?ref=opinion&_r=0 ; Dmitri K. Simes, "And the Winner in Ukraine Is... China," *The National Interest*, March 12, 2014, <http://nationalinterest.org/commentary/the-winner-ukraine-ischina-10034>.

About the Authors

Andreas Herberg-Rothe, Dr. habil., is a permanent lecturer in the faculty of social and cultural studies at the University of Applied Sciences, Fulda, and was a private lecturer of Political Science at the Institute for Social Sciences, Humboldt-University Berlin (up to 2012). He was an associate of the Oxford Leverhulme Programme "The changing character of War" (2004-2005) and convener (together with Hew Strachan) of the conference "Clausewitz in the 21st century" (Oxford 2005). He was a visiting fellow at the London School of Economics and Political Science, Centre for international Studies (2005-2006).

Christopher Coker, PhD, is Professor of International Relations at the London School of Economics and Head of Department. He is also Adjunct Professor at the Norwegian Staff College. He was a NATO Fellow in 1981 and served two terms on the Council of the Royal United Services Institute. He is a serving member of the Washington Strategy Seminar at the Institute for Foreign Policy Analysis (Cambridge, Mass.), the Black Sea University Foundation, and the Moscow School of Politics and the IDEAS Advisory Board. He is a member of the Academic Board of the Czech Diplomatic Academy. He was a Visiting Fellow of Goodenough College in 2003-4. He is a member of the Executive Council for the Belgrade University International Summer School for Democracy and also President of the Center for Media and Communications of a Democratic Romania.

Prof. Dr. Harald Müller is the executive director of the Peace Research Institute Frankfurt (PRIF) and professor of International Relations at Goethe University Frankfurt. His research areas include questions of world order, justice in international relations, as well as arms control and disarmament. He has been a member of German delegations to the NPT Review Conferences from 1995 onwards, served as a member and chair of the UN Secretary General's Advisory Board on Disarmament Matters, and was a member of the IAEA Expert Group on Multilateral Nuclear Arrangements. He is vice president of the EU Consortium for Non-Proliferation and Disarmament and a Member of the Board of Directors of the Cluster of Excellence at Goethe University "The Formation of Normative Orders." His most recent book is "Norm Dynamic in Multilateral Arms Control" (edited with Carmen Wunderlich, The University of Georgia Press 2013).

Dr. Carsten Rauch is a research fellow at the Peace Research Institute Frankfurt (PRIF) and at Goethe University Frankfurt. His research interests include IR theories in general and power transition theory in particular, the rise and fall of great powers, revisionism in the international system as well as Indian foreign policy. His most recent book is "Das Konzept des friedlichen Machtübergangs [The Concept of Peaceful Power Transition]" (Nomos 2014, German).

Namrata Goswami, PhD, is a research fellow at the Institute for Defence Studies and Analyses, New Delhi. Dr. Goswami completed her doctorate from Jawaharlal Nehru University in 2005 on the topic "Just War Theory and Humanitarian Intervention: A Comparative Case Study of East Pakistan and Kosovo." She was a Senior Fellow at the United States Institute of Peace (USIP), Washington, DC, from October 2012 to June 2013; Visiting Fellow at the South Asia Institute, University of Heidelberg (November–December 2010); the International Peace Research Institute, Oslo (PRIO), August 2006 to July 2010; and a Visiting Fellow at the Center for Dialogue, La Trobe University, Melbourne from April to August 2009. She is a recipient of the Fulbright-Nehru Senior Research Fellowship, 2012-2013.

Pang, Zhongying, is a distinguished professor of International Relations at the School of Asia-Pacific Studies, Sun Yat-sen (Zhongshan) University, Guangzhou, China. He was a professor of International Relations at several Chinese universities including Beijing-based Renmin University and Tianjin-based Nankai University. He is currently running a center for the comparative study of international relations theories. His major research projects include

China, Europe, and the US in Global Governance and the Evolution of Chinese Foreign Policy. Pang graduated from China's Nankai University with a BA in economics, UK's University of Warwick with MA in Politics and International Studies, and China's Peking University with PhD in International Relations. He served in both the China Institute of International Studies (CIIS) and the Chinese Embassy in Indonesia. He is a Visiting Fellow at the Brookings Institution in Washington, DC and a Guest Researcher/Professor at the Peace Research Institute Frankfurt (PRIF) and the Goethe University Frankfurt.

Antulio Echevarria II, PhD, became the Editor of the US Army War College Quarterly, *Parameters*, in February 2013. Prior to that, he was the Director of Research for the US Army War College. Dr. Echevarria is the author of *Reconsidering the American Way of War* (Georgetown University Press, 2014); *Clausewitz and Contemporary War* (Oxford University Press, 2007); *Imagining Future War* (Praeger Securities International, 2007); and *After Clausewitz* (University Press of Kansas, 2001). He has also published extensively in scholarly and professional journals on topics related to military history and theory and strategic thinking. Dr. Echevarria is a graduate of the US Military Academy, the US Army Command and General Staff College, the US Army War College, and was a Visiting Research Fellow at Oxford University. He holds M.A. and Ph.D. degrees in history from Princeton University, and is currently working on a book on military strategy for Oxford University Press.

Artyom Lukin, PhD, is currently Associate Professor of International Relations and Deputy Director for Research at the School of Regional and International Studies, Far Eastern Federal University (FEFU) in Vladivostok, Russia. Lukin is an expert of the Russian International Affairs Council. Lukin holds a master's degree in International Relations and a PhD in Political Science from Far Eastern National University. His main research interests are international relations and international political economy in the Asia-Pacific and Northeast Asia; Russian foreign policy; Russia's engagement with the Asia-Pacific; and social, political, and economic processes in the Russian Far East. Lukin has authored and co-authored over 50 scholarly publications in Russian and

English. He has been involved in numerous research and publication projects both in Russia and abroad.

Andrey Gubin, PhD, is Head of Research Programs for the Russian Far East, Russian Institute of Strategic Studies (Vladivostok, Russia); Associate Professor, School of Regional and International Studies, Far Eastern Federal University. He holds MA in International Relations (Far Eastern National University, 2002) and Ph.D. in Political Science (Khabarovsk State Technical University, 2004). His main research interests are national security issues; international military cooperation; WMD non-proliferation; local and regional conflicts; Russian Far East development; Russian foreign policy. Gubin has authored and co-authored over 20 scholarly publications in Russian and English. He is a regular contributor to online publications, including Russian International Affairs Council (russiancouncil.ru) and Russian Institute for Strategic Studies (riss.ru), as well as the Vladivostok media.

References

Badie, Bertrand, La Diplomatie de Connivence - Les Dérives Oligarchiques du Système International (Paris: Découverte 2011).

Berghahn, Volker R. and Wilhelm Deist, Rüstung im Zeichen der wilhelminischen Weltpolitik: Grundlegende Dokumente 1890 - 1914 (Düsseldorf: Droste 1988).

Clark, Christopher, The Sleepwalkers: How Europe Went to War in 1914 (London: PENGUIN BOOKS LTD 2012).

Elleman, Bruce A., Stephen Kotkin and Clive H. Schofield (eds), Beijing's power and China's borders: Twenty neighbors in Asia (Armonk, N.Y: M.E. Sharpe 2012).

Feldman, Noah, Cool War: The Future of Global Competition (New York: Random House 2013).

Feng Yongpin, "The Peaceful Transition of Power from the UK to the US", Chinese Journal of International Politics 1/1 (2006), 83–108.

Fingar, Thomas, "Worrying about Washington: China's Views on the US Nuclear Posture," The Nonproliferation Review 18/1 (2011), 51–68.

Fischer, Fritz, Griff nach der Weltmacht: die Kriegszielpolitik des kaiserlichen Deutschland 1914/18 (Düsseldorf: Droste 1967).

Foot, Rosemary and Andrew Walter, China, the United States, and global order, 1. publ (Cambridge et al.: Cambridge University Press 2011).

Fukuyama, Francis, The End of History and the Last Man (London: Hamilton 1992).

Ganguly, Sumit and William R. Thompson, Asian rivalries: Conflict, escalation, and limitations on two-level games (Stanford, CA: Stanford University Press 2011).

Geis, Anna, Harald Müller and Niklas Schörnig, "Liberal democracies as militant 'forces for the good': a comparative perspective," in Anna Geis, Harald Müller and Niklas Schönig (eds), The militant face of democracy: Liberal forces for good (Cambridge: Cambridge University Press 2013), 307–44.

Geiss, Imanuel, Der lange Weg in die Katastrophe: Die Vorgeschichte des Ersten Weltkriegs ; 1815 - 1914 (München et al.: Piper 1990).

Gilboy, George J. and Eric Heginbotham, Chinese and Indian strategic behavior: Growing power and alarm (Cambridge et al.: Cambridge University Press 2012).

Goldstein, Avery, "First Things First. The Pressing Danger of Crisis Instability in U.S.-China Relations," International Security 37/4 (2013), 49–89.

Hillgruber, Andreas, Bismarcks Außenpolitik, Rombach-Hochschul-Paperback 46, 1. Aufl (Freiburg: Rombach 1972).

Jaschob, Lena, Status, Recognition and Global Political Dreams. The German Kaiserreich and its Naval Programme before World War I, Paper prepared for the 55th International Studies Association Convention, March 26th - 29th (Toronto 2014).

Jervis, Robert, "From Balance to Concert: A study of International Security Cooperation," World Politics 38/1 (1985), 58–79.

Jervis, Robert, "A Political Science Perspective on the Balance of Power and the Concert," The American Historical Review 97/3 (1992), 716–24.

Kagan, Korina, "The Myth of the European Concert: The Realist-Institutionalist Debate and Great Power Behavior in the Eastern Question, 1821–41," Security Studies 7/2 (1997), 1–57.

Kagan, Robert, The Return of History and the End of Dreams (London: Atlantic Books 2008).

Kay, John, Obliquity: why our goals are best achieved indirectly (London: Profile 2011).

Kennedy, Paul M., The Rise and Fall of the Great Powers-Economic Change and Military Conflict from 1500 to 2000 (New York, NY: Random House 1987).

Kugler, Jacek and Douglas Lemke (eds), Parity and War - Evaluations and Extensions of the War Ledger (Ann Arbor, MI: University of Michigan Press 1996).

Kupchan, Charles, How Enemies Become Friends - The Sources of Stable Peace (Princeton, NJ: Princeton Univ. Press 2010).

Kupchan, Charles A. and Clifford A. Kupchan, "Concerts, Collective Security, and the Future of Europe," International Security 16/1 (1991), 114–61.

Le Mière, Christian, "Anti-access/Area denial and the South China Sea," paper presented at the Fourth International South China Sea Workshop, 19-21 November, Ho Chi Minh City, Vietnam (Ho Chi Minh City, Vietnam 2012).

Lebow, Richard N., Archduke Franz Ferdinand lives!: A world without World War I (Basingstoke: Palgrave Macmillan 2014).

Lebow, Richard N., A Cultural Theory of International Relations (Cambridge et al.: Cambridge University Press 2008).

Maddison, Angus, "Historical Statistics of the World Economy: 1-2006 AD," <http://www.ggdc.net/maddison/Historical_Statistics/horizontal-file_02-2010.xls>.

Mitzen, Jennifer, Power in concert: The nineteenth-century origins of global governance (Chicago, London: University of Chicago Press 2013).

Müller, Harald, Daniel Müller, Konstanze Jüngling and Carsten Rauch, Ein Mächtekonzert für das 21. Jahrhundert – Blaupause für eine von Großmächten getragene multilaterale Sicherheitsinstitution, HSFK-Report 1/2014 (Frankfurt am Main: Hessische Stiftung Friedens- und Konfliktforschung 2014).

Müller, Harald and Carsten Rauch, "Managing Power Transition with a 'Concert of Powers?'" paper prepared for presentation at the ISA Annual Convention 2011: March 16-19 (Montreal 2011).

Müller, Harald and Rauch, Carsten, "Machtübergangsmanagment durch ein Mächtekonzert. Plädoyer für ein neues Instrument zur multilateralen Sicherheitskooperation," in: Zeitschrift für Friedens- und Konfliktforschung, forthcoming 2015.

Nirmala, Devi, T. and A. Subramanyam Raju, India and Southeast Asia: Strategic convergence in the twenty-first century (New Delhi: Manohar Publishers & Distributors 2012).

O'Neil, Andrew, Asia, the US and extended nuclear deterrence: Atomic umbrellas in the twenty-first century (London, New York: Routledge, Taylor & Francis Group 2013).

Organski, A. F.K. and Jacek Kugler, The War Ledger (Chicago et al.: University of Chicago Press 1980).

Organski, A. F.K., World Politics (New York, NY: Knopf 1958).

Rasler, Karen and William R. Thompson, "Strategic rivalries and complex causality in 1914," in Jack S. Levy and John A. Vasquez (eds), The outbreak of the First World War: Structure, politics, and decision-making (Cambridge: Cambridge University Press 2014), 65–87.

Rauch, Carsten, Das Konzept des friedlichen Machtübergangs: Die Machtübergangstheorie und der weltpolitische Aufstieg Indiens (Baden-Baden: Nomos 2014).

Röhl, John C. G., From Bismarck to Hitler: The problem of continuity in German history (London: Longman 1970).

Schroeder, Paul W., "The 19th Century International System: Changes in the Structure," World Politics 39/1 (1986), 1–25.

Schroeder, Paul W., Austria, Great Britain, and the Crimean War: The destruction of the European concert (Ithaca, NY: Cornell University Press 1972).

Schroeder, Paul W., The Transformation of European Politics 1763-1848 (Oxford: Clarendon Press 1994).

Schroeder, Paul W., System, Stability, and Statecraft (Houndmills-Basingstoke: Palgrave Macmillan 2004).

Schroeder, Paul W., "Did the Vienna Settlement Rest on a Balance of Power?" The American Historical Review 97/3 (1992), 683–706.

Schulz, Matthias, Normen und Praxis - Das europäische Konzert der Großmächte als Sicherheitsrat, 1815 - 1860 (München: Oldenbourg 2009).

Slantchev, Branislav L., "Territory and Commitment: The Concert of Europe as Self—Enforcing Equilibrium," Security Studies 14/4 (2005), 565–606.

Snyder, Jack, Myths of empire - domestic politics and international ambition, Cornell studies in security affairs (Ithaca et. al: Cornell University Press 1991).

Stevenson, David, Armaments and the coming of war: Europe, 1904 - 1914 (Oxford: Clarendon Press 1996).

Tammen, Ronald L., Jacek Kugler, Douglas Lemke, Allan C. Stamm, III, Mark Abdollahian, Carole Alsharabati, Brian Efrid and A. F.K. Organski, Power Transitions: Strategies for the 21st Century (New York, NY: Seven Bridges Press 2000).

The 21st Century Concert Study Group, A Twenty-First Century Concert of Powers: Promoting Great Power Multilateralism for the Post-Transatlantic Era (Frankfurt am Main: Peace Research Institute Frankfurt 2014).

Ullrich, Volker, Die nervöse Grossmacht - Aufstieg und Untergang des deutschen Kaiserreichs 1871 - 1918 (Frankfurt am Main: Fischer 1997).

van Evera, Stephen, "The Cult of the Offensive and the Origins of the First World War," in Steven E. Miller, Sean M. Lynn-Jones and Stephen van Evera (eds), Military strategy and the origins of the First World War. Revised and Expanded Version (Princeton, NJ: Princeton University Press 1991), 59–108.

White, Hugh, The China choice: Why America should share power (Collingwood, Vic: Black Inc. 2012).

Williamson, Samuel R. Jr., "July 1914 revisited and revised: the erosion of the German paradigm", in Jack S. Levy and John A. Vasquez (eds), The outbreak of the First World War: Structure, politics, and decision-making (Cambridge: Cambridge University Press 2014), 30–62.

Yao Yunzhu, "China's Perspective on Nuclear Deterrence," Air and Space Power Journal 24/1 (2010), 27–30.

Image sources:

Barlach, Ernst, "Das Wiedersehen,"
<http://commons.wikimedia.org/wiki/File:Ernst_Barlach_Das_Wiedersehen_1926_Mahagoni-2.jpg>.

"Soldier releasing messenger pigeon from tank, World War I,"
<http://i.telegraph.co.uk/multimedia/archive/02788/ww1-pigeon-tank_2788228b.jpg>.

Barlach, Ernst, "Moses,"
<http://commons.wikimedia.org/wiki/File:Ernst_Barlach_Moses_1919_Eichenholz-4.jpg>.

"British soldiers eating at the Battle of the Somme, World War I,"
<http://news.bbcimg.co.uk/media/images/74268000/jpg/_74268552_q_001580_iwm_highres.jpg>

Barlach, Ernst, "Magdeburger Ehrenmal,"
<http://en.wikipedia.org/wiki/Ernst_Barlach#Seeking>.

"German soldiers on a battlefield, World War I," <https://europeana1914-1918.s3.amazonaws.com/attachments/1113/539.1113.original.jpg?1303062344>

"Indian soldiers in a trench, World War I,"
<http://www.usiofindia.org/Projects/View/?pid=72>.

"Dedication of World War I memorial, Shanghai,"
<http://blog.lareviewofbooks.org/chinablog/chinas-forgotten-world-war/>.

"American soldiers in Verdun, World War I," <
<http://commons.wikimedia.org/wiki/File:USA_infantry_Verdun_WWI.jpg>.

Barlach, Ernst, "Der Rächer,"
<http://commons.wikimedia.org/wiki/File:Ernst_Barlach_Der_R%C3%A4cher_1922_Lindenholz-1.jpg>.

Index

1914..8-9, 14-16, 19-21, 24, 28-29, 33-35, 41-43, 45, 47-48, 51, 58-60, 66, 70-71, 73, 77-78, 80- 81, 101, 121-122, 125-134, 137-138, 157

A

Afghanistan..12, 14, 98, 109, 112, 116
aggressor..20
ally...............................50, 53, 66, 74, 93, 103, 125, 131, 137-138, 150-151, 154, 160
alliances.......................20, 48, 58, 73, 91, 94-95, 97, 99, 106, 125, 151, 155-156, 160
America...8, 22, 36, 54, 56-57, 78, 97, 102-103, 109, 111-113, 121-122, 127, 142-143, 145, 149, 151, 156-157, 161
American..7-8, 26, 29, 31, 35-37, 52, 54, 58, 67, 80, 94, 96, 99, 105, 110-111, 118, 122, 125, 127, 142, 145, 150-151, 155, 158, 161
anarchy..13, 43
Angell, Norman..19, 20-26, 34
anniversary, one hundredth of World War I...8, 154
Arendt, Hannah...16
arms race...7, 13, 31, 48, 51, 54, 56, 58, 121-126, 128-134
Asia..........................8, 15-16, 36, 41, 54, 56-57, 59, 61, 73-81, 85-89, 91, 93-94, 96-99, 101-104, 106-119, 121-122, 126, 132, 134, 137-141, 143-146, 148-152, 154-161
 conflicts in...8, 14, 101
 rise of..7
Athens...8
Atlantic...21-22, 37, 70, 83, 156
Austria-Hungary......20, 36, 42, 47-51, 67, 80, 126-127, 138, 140-141, 147-148, 151, 154
autocracy...24

B

Balkan...28, 50, 66, 141, 148, 160
believe...27- 29, 32, 34, 95, 99, 101, 125
biographical...27, 29, 33-34

Bismarck..29, 47, 122

C

challenger..43- 45, 47, 60, 64, 71
   challenge..45, 48, 52, 57, 64, 75-76, 103, 107, 109-110, 117, 123, 130, 143, 150, 156-157, 160
change..7, 10, 13, 28, 37, 41, 43-44, 47, 55, 64-65, 67, 76, 83, 91, 94, 98, 107, 109, 114, 117, 125, 127, 132, 134, 141, 145, 151, 161
China 8, 10, 13, 15, 19, 35- 37, 41, 43, 46, 51-65, 69- 71, 73- 99, 101-119, 122-124, 126, 137-158, 160-161
   Beijing...8, 36, 41, 46, 54-55, 59, 102-103, 105-106, 108- 110, 112-113, 115, 117, 122-123, 137-138, 142-146, 148- 157, 160
   East China Sea...76, 79, 80, 91, 123, 144-145
   South China Sea......38, 59, 61-62, 78, 82, 86, 91-92, 98, 106, 115, 123, 142, 147-148
choice..31, 35, 54, 73, 75-77, 102, 107, 111, 156
   China's choice..73- 75, 101-102, 117- 119
rational..32- 34, 36
   utility-maximizing..32
Clausewitz..9, 13
Clinton, Hillary..8, 122-123
communication..71, 81, 92, 95, 134, 159
   intercultural..15
community...10-11, 14, 94, 114, 152-153
complex, complexity......................21, 33, 46-48, 51-52, 59, 63, 111, 118, 130, 144, 151
Concert of Powers..............41-42, 63, 64, 69-70, 101-103, 107-108, 114, 116-119, 161
conflicts..........7, 11-13, 42, 46-48, 51, 60, 64-65, 68, 83, 95, 99, 101, 110, 140, 158, 160
   dynamics..42
   low-intensity..12, 159
   military..10, 15
consequentialist..29
containment, to contain................................30, 36, 53, 58, 62, 65-66, 75, 85, 87-88, 103, 106, 110-111, 122-124, 143, 145, 161
conventions..21

cooperation....................37, 54, 59, 66, 68, 78, 86, 91-93, 95-97, 99, 105, 110-117, 123

crisis..10, 19, 21, 31, 50, 53, 57, 59-60, 62-63, 65, 70, 98, 109, 114-115, 128, 145-146, 153-154, 157, 160

   July crisis 1914..20, 35, 133

cultural...10-12, 15-16, 29-30, 34, 42, 65, 69, 81, 105, 134

D

defeat..9, 11, 29, 83, 89, 144, 146

defense...28, 50, 55, 75-77, 85-86, 89-90, 92-93, 95, 97-98, 106-107, 116, 122- 124, 126, 128, 130, 139, 145, 149, 157-158

   defensive...50-52, 56, 58, 82

democracy...24, 30, 53, 57, 62, 70, 73, 99, 105

   democratize...36

deterrence...7, 57-58, 63, 70, 91, 124-126, 132-134, 147

   deter..21, 57, 124, 128, 133, 157

   deterrent..56, 128

E

economy......22, 32, 52, 73, 75, 77-78, 82, 84, 92, 102, 109, 124, 133, 142, 150, 156-157

   economic.........7, 10, 20-22, 24, 31-32, 35, 38, 53, 58, 65, 73, 75-84, 87, 91, 96, 102, 105-106, 109, 114-115, 123, 125, 130, 132, 134, 141-143, 149-150, 154, 156, 159-160

   economies..21, 32, 37, 41, 123

   political economy...22, 24

emotion..26

Empires...9

England...9, 23-24, 34, 42, 129, 140

   British Empire...23-24, 128

   London...20-21, 23, 26, 28, 30-33, 41, 45, 47, 49, 57, 67, 70, 109, 121, 124, 126-127, 129-131, 143, 153, 161

   the UK...24, 44-45

enthusiasm...24, 33, 57, 70, 103

   before 1914..132

escalation..9, 10, 13, 15, 42, 57, 59, 62-63, 79, 134, 146
ethnic..12, 139
Eurasia...137-138, 151, 160-161
Europe.....................8, 12, 14-15, 21-22, 24, 26, 29, 41-42, 45, 48-49, 51, 54, 64, 66-68, 76, 78, 81, 101-103, 115, 121, 128-129, 132, 137-141, 143, 154, 156, 158, 160-161
European..7-9, 12, 19, 21, 23-24, 35, 41-42, 47, 49-50, 64-71, 101, 108, 130, 139-141, 153, 161
   colonization..7-8, 13
exceptionalism, American..34, 37

F

Ferdinand, Archduke of Austria..35, 70, 80
finance...21
   financial...21-22, 31, 73, 114-115, 159
   financial crisis..31, 98, 109, 114-115
Fischer, Fritz...41, 47
France..................9, 20, 28-29, 42, 45, 47-50, 66, 121, 125-129, 132-133, 140, 146-147
   French..15, 28, 49-51, 80, 126, 128-129, 131, 139
   Paris..48, 68

G

GDP...45-46, 77, 149-150, 160
General...9, 30
General Staff...30, 92
geopolitics...13, 84, 99, 137, 153, 160
   geopolitical..54, 96, 142-143, 147, 150-151, 156, 160
Germany...20, 22-25, 28-30, 36, 45, 47-51, 60, 64, 78, 80, 117, 121, 125-134, 138-143, 146-148, 152, 154-155
   Berlin..25, 45, 49, 143, 154, 157
   German Empire..9, 10, 141
   German Reich..47-49, 131, 133

globalization...........10-11, 13, 15, 35
    global...........11-12, 22, 41-43, 60, 64, 68, 76, 78, 81, 85, 88, 98, 101, 109, 117, 119, 122, 128, 131, 138, 142, 150, 156
    globalized...........10, 13, 104

H

Habsburg Empire...........9
Hegel...........15
hegemony...........7-8, 36, 55, 103, 105, 109, 117, 150, 160
    hegemonic...........11, 60, 65, 107, 111, 116, 119, 149
hierarchy...........43, 68
history...........7-8, 15-16, 27, 29, 33-34, 37-38, 42, 47, 51-52, 63, 70, 74, 77, 80, 82, 84, 122, 139, 142
    progress...........11, 15, 23-24, 86, 94
    repetition of...........7, 14, 80
Hobbes, Thomas...........11, 16
Huntington...........12, 111, 121

I

identity...........9, 11, 74, 79, 148
illusion...........20-21, 24-25, 124
imperialism...........141
    imperialistic...........140
India...........13, 15, 41, 46, 51-57, 61-62, 65, 69, 73, 79, 82-99, 103-104, 115-117, 140-141, 143, 146-147, 150, 156-157
    New Delhi...........55-56, 91, 96, 146-147, 156-157
interconnection...........35, 57, 59, 63
interdependence...........20-21, 35, 77, 80, 99, 142-143, 149, 159
irrational...........32
    irrationality...........30
isolation...........35, 38, 97, 106

J

James, William 19, 26
Japan 36, 46, 52-53, 56, 59, 61-62, 64, 74, 76-77, 79, 91-94, 97-98, 103, 106-107, 112-113, 116-117, 121, 123, 126-128, 130, 138-141, 143-146, 149-150, 152, 156-157

    Tokyo 16, 92, 102, 144, 146, 156-157

K

Kagan, Robert 12, 70
Kaplan, Robert 11, 142

L

leadership 37, 48, 50, 52-53, 60-61, 76, 83, 102, 104, 108, 110, 113, 115-116, 122, 160
    global leadership 36, 85
Lee Kuan Yew 37
legitimacy 12, 14, 73, 82, 99
    illegitimate 37
    legitimate 14, 69, 111
liberalism 22-24
    liberal 11, 20, 24-26, 30, 34, 57, 95-96

M

MacNamara, Robert 10
market 21-24, 31, 35, 105, 129, 142, 149, 151
militarism 26
models
    computer models 28, 33
    economic models 33
modernity 140

modern...10, 15, 24, 27-28, 42, 64-65, 67-70, 90, 97, 108, 117, 121-122, 124-125, 127, 131-132, 138-140, 149, 154, 157, 160
   reactionary modernism...30
morality...14, 21
multilateral...........................14-15, 42, 64-65, 68-69, 78, 109, 113, 115, 152, 161

N

national interests...8, 63, 152
nationalism...20, 24, 37, 48, 98, 139-140, 149
navy, navies...........................30, 56, 61, 92, 118, 126-127, 129-130, 141, 143-144

O

Obama, Barack...75, 86-87, 108-112, 122, 124
offense, offensive...28, 49-50, 56-58, 76, 121, 133, 157, 159
order
   disintegration...12-13
   international order...43-44, 47, 64, 81, 91, 96, 110, 138, 140, 160

P

Pacific...78, 86, 93, 99, 101, 103, 109-111, 113-119, 121, 123-124, 127, 130, 134, 137, 141-146, 148, 153-158, 161
Pakistan...........................13, 53, 56-57, 61-62, 84, 89, 94-95, 115, 141, 147, 150, 158
paradigm...13, 47, 87
passions...19, 26, 37, 148
   sentiment...23
patriotic...24
peace...12, 16, 19-20, 22-25, 35, 42, 51, 64, 66, 70-71, 78, 85, 95, 101, 106-108, 112, 117, 119, 132-133, 143
philosophy...29, 61
   philosophies...24

polarity

    multi-polarity 41, 118, 155

    uni-polarity 118, 155

policy 9, 13, 30, 54, 56, 58, 61, 68, 74, 77, 83, 85, 90, 93-94, 102-108, 110-111, 115-117, 124, 126, 155

politics 9, 12-13, 16, 19, 41, 47-49, 53, 66, 69, 73-74, 78, 81, 84, 91-92, 95, 97, 105, 108-109, 137-138, 144, 154, 161

    political 7-12, 14-15, 19, 22-25, 31, 33-35, 48, 50, 52-53, 62, 67-69, 74-76, 81, 90, 103, 105, 108, 116, 123-124, 132-134, 141, 144, 154, 158, 160

power

    constellations 41, 47, 58

    power shift 41, 43

    transition theory 41-46

    power politics 12-13

    powers

        declining powers 7, 10

        emerging powers 10, 36, 112

        rising powers 46, 63, 70, 97

private 12

    privatization 11

    privatized 11-12

Putin, Vladimir 52, 54, 154-155

R

rationality 7, 26, 32-33

    rational actor 19, 31

reality 25, 27, 29, 33-34, 91, 103, 144

reason 9, 20-21, 25, 27, 29, 33, 36-37, 64, 80, 145

recognition 7-9, 13, 15, 49, 52, 68, 85

religion 10, 13

respect 7, 15, 26, 35, 37, 67, 69, 102, 110, 113

revisionism 47-49, 52-53, 58, 65, 106-107, 113, 141, 149

risk 8, 10, 27-28, 34-35, 53, 63, 107, 129, 130, 138, 145, 148, 156, 159

Russia..9, 13, 15, 20, 28, 36, 41-42, 45-52, 54-57, 59, 61, 65-66, 69-70, 79, 103, 105-106, 113, 115-117, 121, 125-129, 132-133, 137, 140-141, 143, 147-148, 150-158, 160, 161

    Moscow..14, 48, 54, 59, 65, 70, 137-138, 150-154, 156, 158

    Tsarist..42

S

Schmitt, Carl...16
self-destruction...8-9, 12
self-interest...21, 31
Serbia..36, 47-48, 50, 141
Social Darwinism...20, 22-23, 26, 50, 57, 58
socialism..24
society...10, 14, 23-24, 27, 29, 38
    societal..15, 33
Sombart, Werner...22
Sparta..8
Spencer, Herbert..20, 22
stakeholder..82
    responsible stakeholder...36
state
    failed state...12-13
    statesmen..35, 160
strategy......................9, 49, 56, 83, 87, 91, 94, 107, 122, 124-125, 133, 155, 156, 160
    strategic...................11, 50, 53-55, 57, 73-77, 82-86, 88, 90-91, 93-96, 99, 102-103, 105-106, 109, 111, 115, 122, 125, 130, 134, 137, 140-142, 146-153, 155-157, 160-161
    strategies..7, 9-10, 15, 20, 61-62, 125, 132, 134
struggle...11, 15, 22-23, 54, 130, 133-134, 141
    for existence...23
subjectivity, incalculable..31
symmetrical..11, 15
system, international..15, 38, 43, 45, 74, 96-97, 113, 137, 141, 155-156

T

Taiwan..37
Taliban..12
Thucydides..8, 112
trade..20, 26, 75, 86, 96, 115, 141-143, 149, 159
trauma...8
Turkish Empire...9

U

Ukraine..13, 54, 58, 65, 70, 153-154, 158, 160-161
US 8, 10, 12, 15, 19, 30-31, 36-38, 41, 44-47, 52-57, 61-63, 73-81,
   84-89, 91, 93-94, 97-98, 101-104, 106-119, 129, 140-147, 149-152, 156-157, 160-161
   Washington..........................14, 41, 46, 52, 54, 55, 57, 61, 70, 86, 93, 103, 108, 109,
   110, 112, 113, 122, 123, 124, 125, 129, 139, 143, 145, 146, 147, 148, 155, 156, 161

V

values...11, 14
victory...11, 29, 43, 44, 126-127
   victor...11, 19
Vietnam..36, 53, 56, 61, 76, 91-92, 94, 106, 117, 123, 141
violence...11-12, 23, 35, 83, 91

W

war
   aims..9, 56, 58, 88, 89
   Cold War....................12, 14, 45, 55, 70, 76-77, 86, 102-103, 117-119, 122, 124, 134
   Cool War...19, 37
   New Wars..11, 14
   Peloponnesian War..8-9

warfare..11-12, 14-15, 121, 158, 159
weapons of mass destruction..8
Weber, Max...12, 22, 24
White, Hugh..16, 102
William II, German Emperor..29
World War I..7-9, 12-13, 19, 30,
    41-42, 47, 56-57, 64, 67, 80-81, 116-117, 137-139, 141-143, 146-147, 150, 156, 160
World War II...7-8, 45, 64, 117, 119, 147
worldview..22

X

Xi Jinping...78, 109, 112, 154

Z

Zhang Wei Wei...15

**AN INTERDISCIPLINARY SERIES
OF THE CENTRE FOR INTERCULTURAL AND EUROPEAN STUDIES**

**INTERDISZIPLINÄRE SCHRIFTENREIHE
DES CENTRUMS FÜR INTERKULTURELLE UND EUROPÄISCHE STUDIEN**

CINTEUS ▪ Fulda University of Applied Sciences ▪ Hochschule Fulda

ISSN 1865-2255

1 *Julia Neumeyer*
  Malta and the European Union
  A small island state and its way into a powerful community
  ISBN 978-3-89821-814-6

2 *Beste İşleyen*
  The European Union in the Middle East Peace Process
  A Civilian Power?
  ISBN 978-3-89821-896-2

3 *Pia Tamke*
  Die Europäisierung des deutschen Apothekenrechts
  Europarechtliche Notwendigkeit und nationalrechtliche Vertretbarkeit einer Liberalisierung
  ISBN 978-3-89821-964-8

4 *Stamatia Devetzi und Hans-Wolfgang Platzer (Hrsg.)*
  Offene Methode der Koordinierung und Europäisches Sozialmodell
  Interdisziplinäre Perspektiven
  ISBN 978-3-89821-994-5

5 *Andrea Rudolf*
  Biokraftstoffpolitik und Ernährungssicherheit
  Die Auswirkungen der EU-Politik auf die Nahrungsmittelproduktion am Beispiel Brasilien
  ISBN 978-3-8382-0099-6

6 *Gudrun Hentges / Justyna Staszczak*
  Geduldet, nicht erwünscht
  Auswirkungen der Bleiberechtsregelung auf die Lebenssituation geduldeter Flüchtlinge in Deutschland
  ISBN 978-3-8382-0080-4

7   *Barbara Lewandowska-Tomaszczyk / Hanna Pułaczewska (Eds. / Hrsg.)*
    Intercultural Europe
    Arenas of Difference, Communication and Mediation
    ISBN 978-3-8382-0198-6

8   *Janina Henning*
    In Dubio Pro Europa?
    An Analysis of the European External Action Structures
    after the Treaty of Lisbon
    ISBN 978-3-8382-0298-1

9   *Claas Oehlmann*
    Europa auf dem Weg zur Recycling-Gesellschaft?
    Die EU-Rohstoffinitiative im Kontext der Strategie Europa 2020
    ISBN 978-3-8382-0401-7

10 *Volker Hinnenkamp / Hans-Wolfgang Platzer (Eds. / Hrsg.)*
    Interkulturalität und Europäische Integration
    ISBN 978-3-8382-0573-1

11 *Vera Axyonova*
    The European Union's Democratization Policy for Central Asia
    Failed in Success or Succeeded in Failure?
    ISBN 978-3-8382-0614-1

12 *Lisa Moessing*
    Lobbying Uncovered?
    Lobbying Registration in the European Union and the United States
    ISBN 978-3-8382-0616-5

13 *Andreas Herberg-Rothe (ed.)*
    Lessons from World War I for the Rise of Asia
    ISBN 978-3-8382-0791-9

14 *Agnieszka Satola*
    Migration und irreguläre Pflegearbeit in Deutschland
    Eine biographische Studie
    ISBN 978-3-8382-0692-9

Sie haben die Wahl:

Bestellen Sie die
Interdisziplinäre Schriftenreihe des Centrums für interkulturelle und europäische Studien
einzeln oder im **Abonnement**

per E-Mail: vertrieb@ibidem-verlag.de | per Fax (0511/262 2201)
als Brief (*ibidem*-Verlag | Leuschnerstr. 40 | 30457 Hannover)

Bestellformular

❏ Ich abonniere die *Interdisziplinäre Schriftenreihe des Centrums für interkulturelle und europäische Studien* ab Band # ____

❏ Ich bestelle die folgenden Bände der *Interdisziplinären Schriftenreihe des Centrums für interkulturelle und europäische Studien*
____; ____; ____; ____; ____; ____; ____; ____; ____; ____

Lieferanschrift:

Vorname, Name ....

Anschrift ....

E-Mail.. | Tel.: ....

Datum .... | Unterschrift ....

Ihre Abonnement-Vorteile im Überblick:

- Sie erhalten jedes Buch der Schriftenreihe pünktlich zum Erscheinungstermin – immer aktuell, ohne weitere Bestellung durch Sie.
- Das Abonnement ist jederzeit kündbar.
- Die Lieferung ist innerhalb Deutschlands versandkostenfrei.
- Bei Nichtgefallen können Sie jedes Buch innerhalb von 14 Tagen an uns zurücksenden.

ibidem-Verlag

Melchiorstr. 15

D-70439 Stuttgart

info@ibidem-verlag.de

www.ibidem-verlag.de
www.ibidem.eu
www.edition-noema.de
www.autorenbetreuung.de